YOUR PSYCHIC ROAD MAP

Have you ever had a hunch that turned out to be accurate? Have you ever known who was telephoning you before you picked up the receiver? Have you ever had a sudden impulse to do—or not do—something, only to discover later that you should have listened to that feeling?

If any of these things has ever happened to you, then you have been using using your psychic ability instinctively. This book builds on that "hunch" level to teach you how to access all of the psychic abilities available to you, including clairvoyance, telepathy, astral travel, psychometry, psychic healing, and communication with animals and spiritual entities.

This book is not about esoteric theories that have no practical application—here you'll learn psychic techniques that can be used every day to solve problems, psychically shield yourself from harm, attain superior listening and reading comprehension—even help psychically "reserve" a great parking space wherever you go!

Think of this book as a simple road map of the psychic landscape. Let it guide you along all of the routes you need to travel in order to fully release and develop your native psychic gifts. If you truly desire a better life for yourself, this may well be the most empowering book you've ever read.

About the Author

William W. Hewitt was a freelance writer and the author of eight books and other materials published by Llewellyn Publications. He spent more than thirty years as a professional writer and editor in the computer, nuclear power, manufacturing, and mining industries, and was professional member of the National Writers Association. He was a certified clinical hypnotherapist and a professional astrologer. He frequently lectured on hypnosis, mind power, self-improvement, metaphysics, and related subjects. After his retirement in 1994, he and his wife travelled extensively together, as a devoted couple enjoying their "golden years." William W. Hewitt passed from this life in November of 2001.

.

PSYCHIC DEVELOPMENT
for BEGINNERS

William W. Hewitt

2004
Llewellyn Publications
St. Paul, Minnesota, USA 55164-0383

FIRST EDITION
Twelfth printing, 2004

Cover design by Tom Grewe
Interior design and editing by Marguerite Krause

Library of Congress Cataloging-in-Publication Data
Hewitt, William W., 1929–
    Psychic development for beginners : an easy guide to releasing & developing your psychic abilities / William W. Hewitt — 1st ed.
        p.   cm.
        ISBN 1-56718-360-3 (pbk.)
        1. Parapsychology. 2. Occultism. 3. Psychics. I. Title.
BF1031.H358   1996
133.8—dc20   95-49697
                                                        CIP

Llewellyn Worldwide does not participate in, endorse, or have any authority or responsibility concerning private business transactions between our authors and the public.

    All mail addressed to the author is forwarded but the publisher cannot, unless specifically instructed by the author, give out an address or phone number.

Llewellyn Publications
A Division of Llewellyn Worldwide, Ltd.
St. Paul, Minnesota 55164-0383, U.S.A.
www.llewellyn.com

Printed in the United States of America

DEDICATION

To Sandra Weschcke and Nancy Mostad, for all the help, advice, and friendship they have extended to me over the years of my association with Llewellyn Publications. They have gone out of their way to help me greatly in many ways.

TABLE OF CONTENTS

An overview of what to expect from the book and from yourself. An overview of psychic ability. Who you are and how
you fit into the scheme of things. Your innate rights and
responsibilities. These matters are explored as preparation for
your psychic training. You are definitely in control of your
own destiny. Tells how can you make your life go the way you
want it to go. One case study of a basic psychic experience.

Defines altered states of consciousness. Discusses how you can
achieve these altered states and use them to direct the enrichment of your life. Takes you on an excursion of your mind.
One exercise.

A series of six exercises to psychically sensitize your seeing,
hearing, touching, smelling, and tasting senses. Four case
studies to demonstrate psychic uses of the senses.

Training your mind to reach psychic levels. Four exercises for
psychically creating colors, shapes, and movement, and then
deepening your mental level to your basic psychic operating
level. One case study.

LIST OF MENTAL EXERCISES

CASE STUDIES

ILLUSTRATIONS

Chapter 1

INTRODUCTION

We all have some innate psychic ability, but most people never develop it or use it.

I am not one of the great psychics you read about in national magazines or see on television. I am just an ordinary person, like you. I taught myself to develop my innate psychic ability, to an at times remarkable degree, and in this book I will pass on to you valuable information and mental exercises that can enable you to do the same for yourself. Throughout the book I will share a number of personal psychic experiences to give you a broader picture of what the psychic world is all about.

You will find that this psychic business is really quite simple and friendly and you can progress as far, or as little, as you choose.

The book is simple and straightforward, not demanding, and does not require any great intellectual ability or special gifted abilities. The only requirement is an open mind and a spirit of adventure.

Throughout the book I intersperse information about the psychic realm with actual psychic experiences (my own and others' of which I have personal knowledge) and with psychic sensitizing exercises for you to perform. Each personal experience and case history is labeled with a number and title.

Have you ever had a hunch that was true or accurate? Have you ever known who was phoning you *before* you picked up the telephone receiver? Have you ever had a sudden feeling enter your mind that you should, or should not, do something — and found out later you should have listened to your feeling?

Have you ever had an experience that you felt you had had before even though you knew you hadn't? This is called *deja vu* and is a valid psychic experience. *Deja vu* can be due to either of the following:

1. You had the same or similar experience in a previous lifetime. All lifetime experiences are in your mind and available to you. Encountering a similar experience in this lifetime can invoke the memory of a previous lifetime experience.
2. Your mind looked ahead in time to the experience and recorded it. Then when you actually encounter the experience, it seems like a replay.

If you have ever experienced anything like these hunches or feelings, you have had the simplest, most basic kind of psychic (sixth sense) experience. In this book we will build on that basic level to enable you to do things you never dreamed possible.

Case #1
Dad's Shell Hole

My father spent eighteen months in the front lines in World War I. Here is a psychic experience he had during a battle.

Dad and eight comrades were huddled in a huge shell hole, seeking protection from the blistering machine gun fire that saturated the air above their heads.

Dad suddenly became uneasy in the shell hole. He had an irresistible urge to get out of there, even though leaving the safety of the hole didn't make any logical sense.

"Don't do it, Shorty," his companions advised. "You will be killed."

Some unseen force drove Dad to crawl out of the hole on his stomach. He knew bullets were flying past only inches above him. He crawled about a hundred yards to the stump of what had once been a large tree, and sat behind it, sheltered from the enemy gun fire.

He turned and gazed back to the place he'd left just as an artillery shell exploded in the old shell hole. All of his comrades were killed.

Dad had listened to his higher mind, and was saved from death.

Always listen to your hunches, that small voice within, and give thanks for them.

There are many things you need to know before beginning actual mental exercises to sharpen and sensitize your sixth (psychic) sense. You need to know more about who you are in the total scheme of things. You need to know a little more about life, choices, and what psychic experiences are.

I hope this book will help you to open up your innate sixth sense and sharpen all of your senses so that you can develop into a practicing psychic, enjoying life to the fullest, as I have done and am still doing. In fact, I hope that you will progress much further than I have.

What you do with the exercises and material in this book is up to you. There are no tests, no homework, no pass/fail grades. This book is exactly what you make of it.

You can go on to make psychic development a way of life for yourself and achieve much, or do just a little — or do nothing. The choice is yours!

Choices, once executed, cannot be erased. This book is dedicated to all of you who execute choices to use your abilities to make the world a better place in which to live and a better place for your having been here.

This book will take you into the dimension of psychic awareness and show you how to use this dimension in constructive ways for the benefit of yourself, others, and, ultimately, our entire society.

The psychic dimension is extremely powerful and useful. It is obtainable by everyone who is willing to exercise self-discipline and spend a small amount of time each day to learn and practice his or her innate psychic ability. Psychic ability is part of everyone's birthright. Initially, you will sensitize your five senses (seeing, hearing, smelling, touching, tasting) because your powerful sixth sense utilizes your sensitized first five senses to enable you to experience the wondrous psychic dimension of your mind.

Psychic power is so effective that it would be irresponsible to launch into developing that power without first having some understanding of yourself, life, interaction with others, responsibility, choices, rights, and much more. These topics will be discussed to ensure your responsible success as a citizen of the universe.

Not everyone will develop full-blown psychic abilities from this book alone. However, you should learn enough to understand how to continue developing your abilities throughout the rest of your life. Other people will experience great psychic growth from this book, simply because they have great innate ability that is already close to their conscious awareness. We are not all equal or identical in our innate psychic ability. Accept that whatever happens, or doesn't happen, is determined by who you are. Also, those who practice more diligently are likely to develop faster and further than those who practice haphazardly or not at all.

Many people know all the "buzz words" associated with psychic phenomena: clairvoyance, clairaudience, astral travel, altered states, telepathy, psychometry, etc. Fewer people really understand what it is all about. That is like knowing the price of everything but the value of nothing.

Although I will give you brief definitions of many of these popular terms, this book is about value, not about neat buzz words that you can use in conversation to try to impress people. This book is intended to enable you to impress yourself, not others.

Use your psychic ability to help yourself and others, not to show off. Psychic ability is about life — your life — not about being the center of attention. Misused psychic ability has a way of crashing down hard on those who misuse it.

A Few Term Definitions

Here are are my definitions of a few terms I use in this book, to help you more easily grasp the exact intent of what is being discussed.

Thought — Thought creates everything. Thought is an energy, and once created can never be destroyed. A basic, unshakable law of physics states that energy, once created, can never be destroyed. Energy can be altered to a different kind of energy, but it can never be destroyed — it always exists somewhere in some form. As a psychic, you will use your thoughts to contact other thoughts in cosmic consciousness. You will use your thoughts to cause things to happen. A word to the wise: be very careful in what you allow yourself to think about. I think you can figure out why.

Psychic Ability — Psychic ability is the ability to gain access to information, energy, or power in cosmic consciousness and to utilize the information, energy, or power you obtain.

Cosmic Consciousness — This is the total intelligence, awareness, creativity, and power within all universes. You are a tiny part of cosmic consciousness, as is every other creature that exists, or ever existed, or ever will exist. Our Creator has given us the privilege of being part of the Creator's domain, which is cosmic consciousness. By exercising our psychic sense, we can interact with various intelligences in cosmic consciousness.

Brain — Your brain is a physical part of your body, essentially a super computer with a fantastic memory. Your brain dies when your body dies. We will discuss how brain function relates to your psychic sense later in the book.

Mind — Your mind is the total intelligence that is YOU. Your mind is not physical, and your mind never dies. Your mind is not your brain. Your mind uses your brain as a communications link between you and other intelligence in cosmic consciousness.

Higher Mind and Superconscious Mind — These are terms I sometimes use to refer to that part of cosmic consciousness that is the communications link between your mind and cosmic consciousness.

Subconscious Mind — This is a part of your mind that utilizes a specific brain wave frequency range for a variety of psychic functions. More on this later.

Entity — This refers to a non-physical intelligent being, a mind without a body, such as a ghost, angel, etc.

Sixth Sense, Intuition, Creative Ability, Psychic Ability (see Chapter 3) — I use all of these terms interchangeably with the same intended meaning.

Your Role

This book is about you, from your personal behavior to how you interact with others and with your environment. It is about how you determine your own destiny; it is about your success or failure. It describes how you can deliberately choose to alter your life for the better, and then make that choice happen.

This book is about your choices and your actions. It is about your responsibilities and your innate power to execute those responsibilities.

This is a how-to book — how to enrich your life and the entire world.

You do make a difference. For better or worse, you make an important, real, measurable difference. You may have heard this before without really understanding it. Perhaps you could benefit by hearing it again, in different words, from a different perspective, and at a different point in your life.

The ideas presented in this book are intended to jingle something deep inside you and get you off dead center. In other words, I hope to give you a mental kick in the rear to propel you into action that will enrich your entire life, from its most simple, mundane moments to the awesome, earth-shaking events.

This book very simply shows you what needs to be done, and shows you how to do it. The actual "doing it," of course, is entirely up to you.

Our world is a society of individual people, and the strength and beauty of this world depends very directly on each of us. You personally influence the soundness of our world in some way.

"You've got to be kidding. I'm just a little old lady on social security. My influence is zip!"

"Get off it, Mac! I drive a taxi in the Big Apple. My biggest influence is in deciding which route to take across Manhattan."

"I'm just a freshman in high school. I can't even get elected class president, let alone accomplish anything really important."

No, I am not mistaken. I am talking about YOU, the little old lady, and YOU, the taxi driver, and YOU, the student. I am addressing every YOU in the world, regardless of social position, intelligence level, economic level, race, religion, color, political bent, or nationality. YOU are all equally important; no one more so, nor less so, than the other. Each of you has power beyond your wildest imagination. Your use or misuse of that power determines whether you prevent the world from being scarred by wars, hunger, crime, suffering, sickness, unkindness, injustice, etc. or whether you aid in scarring the world.

"I've never lifted a finger in anger against any person," you may protest. "Don't blame me for the world's troubles."

First of all, I don't blame anyone. This book is about what is — it is about truth. In truth, there is no blame — truth simply is.

Second, you don't personally have to do something in order to be responsible for an undesirable result. You also must bear responsibility for the result if you refrain from doing something that you could have done.

Remember this axiom: "All that it takes for evil to exist is for good people to do nothing." Hitler brought massive destruction into the world because, for a time, millions of individuals did nothing to stop him. Finally, masses of righteous men and women became so outraged that they fought back and created more destruction in order to stop Hitler. It had to be done, but the truly sad thing is that the situation need not have existed in the first place.

Most of the people in the world are good; all can potentially be good if they so choose. Yet the world is horribly scarred. Why?

Because those who can choose to correct or prevent the problems don't. In all fairness, they don't act because of ignorance. They don't know they have the choice, and they don't know they have the power.

Here and now I tell you: you do have a choice, and you do have the power. This book will explore choices and show you how to develop and exercise your power.

We humans always have a choice about the quality of our lives and about our role in society. Problems often occur because we don't realize that we do have the power to exercise our choices and determine our own destiny.

This is real. This is truth. All you need to do is recognize the truth and use it, flow with it, harmonize with it, embrace it, and in so doing change the world for the better.

Are you completely happy? Probably not. The truth is you do not have to be unhappy.

Is there hatred in the world? Yes. The truth is there doesn't have to be.

Nothing in the world exists without our having caused it, either individually or collectively. Anything in the world can be corrected or changed if we, individually or collectively, decide to act.

Changing the world is fairly simple, but it requires unwavering individual commitment. This book can get you started; the commitment is up to you.

I am going to take you into the awesome realm of psychic awareness and show you how you can create your own reality. I will show you how you can help reshape your life, the lives of others and ultimately the world, even if to only a tiny extent.

Some of the experiences available to you are esoteric, such as telepathic communications, hunches, psychic phenomena and all the others that fall under the general category of paranormal experience. This book deals with these uses of your mind.

Some of the experiences available to you are practical, such as taking the most beneficial action in day-to-day affairs, making better choices in all avenues of your daily life, psychic goal setting, and learning how to flow with energy in such a way as to actually cause improvement in your life in real, measurable ways. It is most important to understand and deal with the fact that we are living this life right now. That is why this book is devoted to practical uses of your mind.

The esoteric and the practical are not that far apart. They are quite compatible, and when you finish the book you will see how these two are blended into one extremely powerful creative force.

Choices

You make hundreds of daily choices about the governing of your life. These choices run the gamut from which pair of shoes to wear and what to eat, to whether or not to seek a new job, how to get the attention of someone you are interested in, and how to budget your money. These personal choices directly, and often immediately, affect you. You are totally responsible for these choices, and you personally reap the results of your choices. If you make a poor choice, you reap an undesirable result. If you make a good choice, you reap a desirable result. It is your choice, and you are responsible.

Wouldn't it be nice if you made more good choices and fewer poor choices? Wouldn't it be nicer still if you made all good choices and no poor choices? Wouldn't it be nice if there were a way to stack the odds for making only good choices in your favor?

Good news! There is a way to stack the odds in your favor, so that you make better choices. In fact, you can go beyond stacking the odds. You can actually make choices and then make them become reality. No longer do you have to hope things will turn out okay; now you can make them turn out okay. This book is devoted to teaching you how to do just that.

Some of your choices will be part of the collective choice of a group of people who are jointly directing their mental energies and making choices for a common goal. This group might consist of members of a family unit jointly planning a vacation. Here you all know each other and have a very personal goal. The outcome of your choice will immediately be felt, and will affect each of you directly and personally.

Still other choices will contribute to the collective choice of a group you don't even know. When you vote for candidate X in a national election, you have made a choice harmonious with the millions of others who also are voting for candidate X. You don't even know the other people who made the same choice. How this choice may or may not affect you is more complex than a personal choice such as whether or not to see a movie today.

These collective-you choices are every bit as important as your individual choices. You are as responsible for your collective-you choices and their results as you are for your individual choices.

The additional good news is that you also can stack the odds in your favor in these collective-you choices. This book will get you started in understanding how.

If you are not pleased with who you are, where you are, what you are doing, or where you seem to be heading, don't think others are responsible. You alone are responsible. You can change any aspect of your life that you really want to change. The key is "really want to." Most people wish things were different, but that is as far as it goes. They do not really want to change strongly enough to cause a change. Mere wishing is not enough. As my late beloved father used to say, "Put your wishes in one hand and put manure in the other. Watch and see which fills up first." If you just rely on wishing, you are going to collect manure in your life. Manure may be good for growing mushrooms, but not for growing good human lives. In a later chapter I will show you how to create a psychic goal bowl to help you achieve what you really want to achieve.

As long as you are willing to advance beyond the wishing stage, a wish is a good beginning for improvement. Take your wish, turn it into a clearly defined constructive dream, release that dream to higher mind for results, and then follow up with the best constructive action possible to make the dream come true, and always hold that dream strongly in your mind as you pursue your actions to create your reality.

What if you have lost your left arm in an auto accident and wish you had the arm back? How can you turn that wish into reality? You cannot literally grow another arm because that is contrary to physical law. Starfish can grow new arms to replace lost ones; human beings cannot. That is universal law. This brings up a very important rule: whatever you want to become reality in your life must be in harmony with universal law. That is the law. That is truth. That is just the way it is.

You might be able to get some sort of artificial arm replacement. Or you might be able to hire someone to help you so that they, in effect, become another arm. But you cannot physically grow another arm. For your wishes to progress to reality, they must follow universal law.

These four elements are necessary for achievement:

1. Have a wish (desire).
2. Create the dream (visualize).
3. Release the dream to higher mind (faith and commitment) while still retaining the visualization.
4. Take constructive action (take control and direct your dream).

Written as a formula this becomes:

Desire + dream + faith + commitment + action = success

We have established the premise that you can change virtually anything in your world that you wish to change, and have
stated some basic conditions for creating change. Now we move
into a different dimension in order to implement the changes
we want.

The dimension we are going to enter is one called *altered
states of consciousness* in the psychic realm.

■ ■

Chapter 2

ALTERED STATE OF CONSCIOUSNESS

Hypnosis is the name for a procedure that enables you to alter your state of consciousness in order to achieve some desirable goal. Meditation is another name for this procedure. Prayer is another name. There are probably a number of other names as well. By whatever name you call it, the procedure works quite well if you understand what you are doing and practice faithfully.

I will dispense with all the other names and just talk about altered states and how you can learn to achieve them and use them in your psychic work.

There are two types of altered state: a harmful one, and a beneficial one.

The harmful altered state is induced by alcohol or drugs. In this state, you are not in control of yourself, even though you have the delusion that you are. You are in physical and mental danger. Your health is endangered. You might, much to your horror, become "possessed" by another intelligent entity. Please do not experiment with this type of mind altering. You have everything to lose, and absolutely nothing to gain. This book does not teach or advocate anything that is harmful.

The highly beneficial altered state is the one that this book is all about. We are designed by our Creator to be capable of naturally altered states of consciousness to use for our benefit. We

experience these altered states every day of our lives quite spontaneously (more on this shortly). What we are going to discuss
is how to achieve the altered state when we want to, and then
use that opportunity to invoke desired changes in our lives.
This beneficial altered state is achieved without the use of any
drugs, medicines, or other substances. It is achieved by using
your natural ability to control your own mind.

The purpose of this book is to enable you to become independent, rather than dependent, and to be completely in control of your own life at all times in concert with the choices you
decide for yourself. No longer do you need to be subjected to
the whims and desires of others. No longer do you need to give
up part of your identity, your dreams, your goals, to satisfy
what someone else wants of you.

Did you ever wonder why some marriages are a bed of
disharmony, contention, unhappiness, and lack of fulfillment,
while other marriages are harmonious, happy, and fulfilling?
Everyone can have a completely satisfactory marriage if they
know how. You have the right to a happy, fulfilling life.

Did you ever wonder why some people are not able to
achieve any measure of success in their work? They hate their
work, or don't understand what is expected of them, or are
always out of tune with the boss. Yet other people seem to
always do the right thing in the right way at the right time.
They like their work, understand what is expected of them, and
are always in tune with the boss. Everyone can have work that
they like and at which they can be successful. You have the
right to enjoyment and success in your work.

Did you ever wonder why some people are always sick? If
something is going around, they get it. If they are in a car accident involving multiple persons, they are the only one injured,

or the most seriously injured. Yet other people rarely, or never, get sick. They are the ones who walk away from accidents uninjured, or do not even have accidents. You don't have to get sick or injured. You have the right to be healthy and free of pain.

Did you ever wonder why some people are always out of step with what is happening? They are in the wrong place at the wrong time. They get on the down elevator when they need to go to the top floor. Yet other people always seem to flow in and out of situations as if they have charmed lives. They are in the right place at the right time. If such a person inadvertently gets on the down elevator, you can bet he or she will find a twenty-dollar bill at the bottom. It is entirely by your own choices that you are either "in tune" or "out of tune." You can program yourself to be always "in tune." You have the right to be "in tune."

Did you ever wonder why a few, selected people have paranormal experiences? They can tune in to other minds. They can obtain information from some mystical source. They can interact intelligently with people who are deceased. They can do things that are often considered miraculous. Yet other people seem unable to walk and chew gum at the same time, let alone engage in paranormal experiences. You have the innate ability to have these paranormal experiences. You have the right to experience the psychic world.

You do have the innate ability to experience all of these things and even much more. You also have the birthright — you do not need someone's permission — to experience happiness, achievement, knowledge, fulfillment, and so forth.

People do not experience this enrichment of their lives because they haven't learned how. They keep trying to swim upstream against the current, instead of learning how to flow with the current and utilize the natural energy patterns that are part of their beings. They don't know that they have these rights and the abilities, so they relinquish them, and experience unhappiness instead.

There is one other important factor in experiencing a full life — responsibility. When you have a right, it can only be realized if you accept your responsibility for the right, and exercise your responsibility to experience it. Having a right is meaningless unless you step up to your responsibility to claim that right.

This book points out your rights and shows you how to develop and use your innate abilities to realize those rights, but the responsibility is yours; what you do with what you learn is your choice. So in addition to rights and innate ability we will be dealing with responsibility and choices, all in relation to the realm of psychic experience.

Hypnosis is often thought of as being the ultimate achievement in the use of the mind to solve problems or achieve goals. A smoker undergoes hypnosis and stops smoking. A person is hypnotized and doesn't feel the pain of surgery. A "loser" is hypnotized and becomes a "winner." What could possibly upstage such spectacular events as this?

Hypnosis certainly is a marvelous, powerful tool. I am a clinical hypnotherapist, and I believe in the tremendous benefits that can be gained through hypnosis. However, I believe that hypnosis is just the beginning, not the ultimate goal. Going into the psychic realm offers experiences and achievement that dazzle the mind. As the late Al Jolson used to say, "You ain't seen nothin' yet!"

The Skyscraper of Your Mind

A skyscraper is a very tall building made of steel, cement, and glass. It has a basement and many floors. There is something different on each floor, and an elevator to quickly transport you to whichever floor you wish to visit.

Your mind is similar to the skyscraper. It has a basement and many floors. Each floor is a different level of conscious, subconscious, and superconscious awareness, knowledge, and ability. Your mind is made of pure, intelligent energy rather than the skyscraper's steel, cement, and glass. Your elevator is your developed ability to go to any level of your mind at will.

Exercise #1

Mental Skyscraper Excursion

Imagine with me now for a few moments.

- Imagine that you are standing in front of an infinitely tall skyscraper that represents your mind.
- Look up. You are unable to see the top of the building; it disappears into the clouds and beyond.
- You know your mind is endless just like this skyscraper.
- Now walk into the ground floor and look around.
- You see many office doors. One is labeled "self-preservation." Others are labeled "food," "shelter," "safety," "procreation." As you look at all of the doors you realize that this ground floor of your mind is concerned with the basic necessities of life and survival. You are very familiar with this floor (level).
- Across the lobby you see two elevator doors side by side. One is labeled "down only" and the other "up only."

- Walk over to the elevator marked "down only" and enter the elevator.
- Allow the elevator to descend to the basement.
- Allow the door to open, but do not leave the elevator. Just peer through the door.
- You see doors labeled "greed," "violence," "hatred," "pride." You can see many more doors with equally undesirable labels. You realize that this is your lower self.
- You realize that you have been to this level many times in the past, and you are all too familiar with this level. You do not like it here.
- You can feel the negative vibrations, and vow never to return.
- Now close the elevator door and lock the entrance to this basement level.
- Drop the key down the crack between the elevator and the elevator shaft. The key immediately falls down the shaft. You are not able to retrieve it. Allow the elevator to return to your ground floor.
- Exit the elevator.
- Turn around and close the door and place a large, powerful, unbreakable lock on the door. You will not use this "down" elevator again.
- Now enter the "up" elevator and allow it to go to your first floor (level).
- Open the unlocked door and walk down the hallway and observe the doors on this first level. One is labeled "dreams," another "hunches." You are familiar with these labeled doors. You have been here before.
- You also see many unlabeled doors; you have not yet experienced what is behind these doors.
- Return to the elevator and go up to the second level.

- The door here is locked. You are unable to see what is on this level.
- You determine in your mind to find a key for the lock so you will one day be able to open the door.
- Return now to your ground floor.
- You realize you have a greater awareness of yourself. You know you have a lower nature which you never again wish to experience. You know you have some awareness of a higher self. You also know that you have hundreds of levels of higher self that you have not yet unlocked.
- You vow to find a way to unlock those higher levels and experience them.
- Walk outside and gaze up once again at the skyscraper of your mind. Note how immeasurably tall it is. You have completed a mini-excursion in your mind; you want more.

We will make extensive use of mental exercises that will enable you to unlock and experience all levels of your higher self at will, thus enabling you to function in the psychic realm.

As you go increasingly higher and higher in your mental sky-scraper you will encounter increasingly sophisticated and eso-teric experiences. At some level, you will satiate all conscious experiences; the next level begins the subconscious. At some higher level of awareness you encounter the superconscious, etc. The only limit on your achievement is the limit you place on it. If you don't want to go beyond the twentieth floor, you won't. The very top floor is total enlightenment, fulfillment, knowledge, and realization.

Getting There

To achieve the higher levels of your mental skyscraper, you must learn to lower your brain operating frequency until you can transport yourself to the necessary level. You do this through simple relaxation and visualization techniques which will be explored extensively in this book.

Your brain frequency fluctuates countless times every day, changing spontaneously as the need arises. The most notable time, familiar to all of us, is when we go to sleep at night. Lay your head on the pillow, close your eyes, and your brain automatically starts cycling down so you can rest, dream, and become rejuvenated. The sleep process is necessary for us to maintain our mental and physical health and balance.

Hans Berger, using an EEG machine in 1929, discovered that when a person's eyes were closed the brain started generating regular waves in the 8 to 12 cycles per second (cps) range. He labeled these brain waves *alpha* waves. Subsequently other types of brain waves were discovered and labeled *theta, beta,* and *delta.* These brain waves have been found to have a correlation to various mental functions, including psychic experience. Experts generally agree on these brain waves and their purpose, but they disagree on the exact boundaries of each kind of wave. One will define alpha as 8 to 12 cps; another as 7 to 14 cps, and so forth. In the next few paragraphs I will present what I believe is a general consensus concerning these brain waves. With this information you can better understand how psychic abilities are a part of everyone's makeup right from birth.

Beta — When we are awake and performing our daily chores, our brain operates primarily in the beta frequency range, from approximately 12 to 15 cycles per second and up, with most activity occurring at approximately 20 to 25 cycles per second. This is our conscious mind. At this level of brain operation, we reason, rationalize, and execute whatever chores we need to do.

Alpha — The alpha range of brain activity occurs at approximately 6 to 14 cycles per second. Here, daydreaming and nocturnal dreaming take place. Most hypnosis also takes place in the alpha range. Some psychic experiences also occur here.

Theta — Between approximately 4 and 8 cycles per second we find the theta state. Our emotional experiences seem to be recorded here. This also is a powerful range from which you can launch into psychic experience.

Delta — Frequencies of less than 4 or 5 cycles per second are encountered in total unconsciousness, the delta state.

Sleep Cycle — When you drift into sleep, your brain quickly cycles out of beta, through alpha and theta, and into delta, where you remain for a short while. Typically, you might make the transition from beta into delta in 30 minutes, then remain in delta for 30 to 90 minutes. At that point, your brain would cycle up into theta, then into alpha where you would dream for a while. After one dream session your brain would cycle back down into theta, then up into alpha for more dreaming. In an eight-hour sleep period, you might spend 30 to 90 minutes in delta, 30 to 60 in theta, and the rest of the time in alpha.

This is an illustrative sleep cycle. It will vary from person to person, and even from night to night with the same person.

The important thing to note is that altered states are natural phenomena. You go through them every day.

Even when you are awake, your brain will frequently dip into alpha and theta for brief periods. For instance, if you hit your finger with the hammer while pounding a nail, your brain dips into theta to record the pain. Or perhaps you are studying and trying to memorize some material. You look off into space to record the material in your brain at alpha.

Achieving Altered States — Quite simply, all you need to do to become a psychic is to learn how to deliberately cause your brain to go into alpha or theta, and how to remain there for as long as you wish without falling asleep. Although easy to describe, these skills take a little effort and discipline to achieve. Also, there is a bit more to becoming a psychic than learning skills. Everything will be covered before the end of the book. The most important thing to remember at this point is that Hans Berger discovered that the brain automatically starts generating alpha waves whenever a person closes her/his eyes. This gives you a giant clue that it isn't going to be all that difficult to achieve a psychic level of mind — you'll just close your eyes and perform some simple relaxation and visualization exercises.

Visualization — The key to achieving theta at will and then using that state to achieve psychic experiences is visualization. A short while ago, I had you take a visual excursion through your skyscraper mind. We will be concerned a great deal with visualizing.

The Gunfighter — To become a good practicing psychic you are going to become a gunfighter with your mind.

In the old west, the gunfighter practiced incessantly until his eyes, instincts, hands, and gun became as one. He got to the point where he did not think at all. He was a finely tuned machine able to act with precision and accuracy, faster than if he had taken the time to think about it.

You must learn to do with your mind what the gunfighter did with his gun. You can get to the point where you'll alter your state of consciousness as fast as the gunfighter's draw. You will lock into the necessary level of your mind as accurately as the gunman aimed at a target. When you become totally at one with yourself, you will be a master. Do not expect to be a master after reading this book. Becoming a master is a lifelong pursuit; perhaps many lifetimes.

This book will teach you to be a psychic gunfighter, so to speak, by showing you how to hone your senses to keen awareness, but the practice is entirely up to you. If you wish to become a mental gunfighter, you must practice, practice, and practice everyday. The mechanism of practice is visualization.

The Mind — The most difficult thing for many people to comprehend is just what the mind is. The most common misconception is that the mind and the brain are the same thing. Not so.

The brain is a physical collection of flesh, nerves, chemicals, blood, and cells, housed in our skull. The brain is like a super computer. It can remember, reason, and perform all sorts of mental wizardry. When our container, our physical body, dies, the brain also dies.

The mind is the total intelligent energy that is us. While we are housed in our physical container, the mind uses our brain. The mind is non-physical; it belongs to the spiritual or psychic world, and it never dies. The mind is who we are.

■ ■

Chapter 3

SHARPENING YOUR FIRST FIVE SENSES

We are born with six senses: Seeing (eyes); Hearing (ears); Touching (skin sensors); Smelling (nose): Tasting (tongue and mouth); and a sixth sense (mind) which might also be called intuition or psychic sense. The sixth sense can be extremely powerful, and yet few people ever develop or use this valuable gift from our Creator.

If the truth be known, most of us haven't developed our other five senses to any great extent, either. We will deal with sensitizing our first five senses now because our sixth sense utilizes all of the other five senses from time to time in addition to using its own mental abilities.

What follows are some suggestions on how to start right now to become more sensitive to external and internal stimuli. The things I suggest take only seconds or minutes and should be practiced until you are satisfied that "tuning in" to stimuli is an innate part of your behavior. Then you won't have to practice consciously because you will have conditioned yourself to be sensitive at all times.

Seeing

Most psychics use sight a great deal in their psychic work. There are two kinds of psychic sight. The first involves seeing images, scenes, or beings inside your own mind. The second involves seeing images, scenes, or beings outside your mind; one example is seeing an apparition (ghost, entity).

I personally have not yet seen an entity, though I have had numerous encounters with them; I sense their presence, communicate with them, and on two occasions have physically felt them touch me, but have not yet physically seen them. I do, however, see images in my mind on the screen inside my head quite often. The next case is an excellent example of psychic sight.

Case #2
Use of Psychic Sight

I had two profound, spontaneous psychic experiences within a few weeks of each other that altered my life forever. The first occurred about two months before the United States lifted the restriction on gold prices (held to about $35 an ounce) and allowed the gold price to float on the world market and seek its own level in a manner similar to the way the stock market floats daily. To the best of my recollection, this was in the early 1970s.

I was the publications manager for a large computer equipment engineering and manufacturing company and had forty-seven people reporting to me. The psychic world was not of any particular interest to me.

One Monday, one of my employees (I'll call him Harry) came into my office to talk about some job-related problem. I was sitting at my desk doing some paperwork. When I looked up to greet him, I had an instantaneous experience, unlike anything I had ever had before.

It was as though a movie projector in the back of my head projected a movie on the inside of my forehead. The movie showed Harry attempting suicide the previous day by swallowing a quantity of pills. I saw him lapse into unconsciousness. Then his wife (I'll call her Rose), a registered nurse, found him and had him rushed to the hospital, where his stomach was pumped. Rose was on the hospital staff, and she was able to stifle any news reports about it. Harry came to work the next day to avoid any suspicions being raised. I saw this whole thing in my head in just a few seconds.

I was so startled that I sat there for a short while, dumbfounded, just staring into space and thinking about it.

Finally, I realized that Harry had been talking to me, and I didn't know what he had been saying.

"I'm sorry, Harry," I muttered, "I am preoccupied. Would you repeat that?"

Harry started to talk, and that movie went off in my head again, giving me an instant replay.

I didn't understand what was happening, but it was too real and vivid for me to ignore. I got up and walked to the door and closed it. Then I pulled up a chair next to Harry.

"Harry, do you have a personal problem that we need to talk about?" I asked.

"No! No! Everything is fine," he said. His sudden visible nervousness told me he was lying.

Then my movie played again. I decided to throw caution to the wind. I asked Harry point blank, "Did you try to take your own life yesterday?"

Harry grew pale and began to weep. I let him get it out of his system.

"How did you know?" he finally managed to say. "Rose called you, didn't she?"

"No, Rose didn't call me. How I know is not important. What is important is ..." I was interrupted in mid-sentence by another movie.

This movie showed Harry using a gun to execute a successful attempt the following Sunday. He had a plan that would not be thwarted.

I finished my interrupted sentence, "... is that you do not go through with your plan on next Sunday."

"My God! How could you possibly know?" He began shaking and weeping again.

When he regained his composure, I began to speak words that were being channeled through me. I could feel the intelligence coming into the crown of my head. I seemed to process the intelligence and speak the words.

"Harry, I know you are feeling a lot of pain, and you want to die. It is your life, and you can choose to die if you want to. You have that right. But you also have another right. That is the right to live, and you have never explored this right. I will make a commitment to you if you will make one to me. Give me two weeks of your life. Do not kill yourself for two weeks. During that time, let me get you on a medical program. Also, I want you to come to my office every afternoon from one until three and we will talk. If you still want to kill yourself after the two weeks are up, go ahead. I promise not to alert anyone or try to stop you. I am not asking much. You have had this pain for forty years. You can bear it for just two more weeks."

"You won't tell?"

"I promise."

"Okay. I'll give it two weeks," he said.

I immediately took Harry to the company doctor who got him started on a therapy program.

When I returned to my office, I wondered what in the world I was going to talk to Harry about when he started coming in for daily chats. Everything I had said to Harry was just a parroting of words I was fed from some intelligence source that I didn't understand. I certainly wasn't equipped by knowledge or training to handle this kind of situation.

My apprehension was put to rest, however, when Harry came in to see me each day. As soon as he closed the door and sat down, my unseen intelligence source provided me with the words. I could feel them enter the crown of my head. Harry and I learned together.

After two weeks, Harry came into tell me his decision.

"Bill," he said, "I am not out of the woods yet. I still have a long way to go. But the furthest thing from my mind is suicide. I want to live. Thank you for helping me explore my right to live."

Epilogue: Harry is still alive and happy today. He raised his children to adulthood, and has found meaning in life. All this because I allowed myself to function as an open psychic channel from higher intelligence.

At the time, of course, I didn't know that that was what I was doing. I had no idea what was going on. After pondering it for a week or so, I dismissed the experience as some sort of inexplicable fluke. Little did I know.

But higher mind wasn't finished with me, as indicated by my second spontaneous psychic experience. I will relate it to you in Case #3, later in this chapter.

Exercise #2

Sensitizing Your Sense of Sight

- At night, with no lights on, look around you and study and identify the shapes you see. Do this in bed, out in your yard, walking the sidewalk in your neighborhood, while camping, etc.
- As you identify each shape, say (either mentally or out loud, as you prefer) "This is what a (name of object) looks like in the dark. I am sensitizing my sight to recognize objects accurately in the dark and under any lighting situation."
- During daylight, at any place or time, take a few seconds to observe what is around you.
- Mentally repeat what you see and say, "I am training my psychic mind to accurately observe my environment at all times."
- Say "I command my subconscious mind to always alert me to everything I need to see for my benefit and protection, so that I may function to my fullest psychic capacity."

The preceding procedure is illustrative. You may use it as is, or you may create your own exercise to achieve the same conditioning of your psychic mind.

This is the kind of exercise you may want to practice every day for a few seconds because it greatly increases your awareness of your environment as well as sensitizing your psychic mind.

You will be amazed to discover how many things exist in your environment of which you were not consciously aware. Good powers of observation are a great asset.

We will be doing a great deal of visualization in future chapters to enhance your vision even further, giving you psychic vision in your head. Visualization is probably the greatest of all abilities in performing psychic work.

Hearing

When you hear something psychically it is called clairaudience. Clairaudience is the ability to hear audible messages from outside the normal range of sources.

Here is a detailed account of my only clairaudience (hearing voices) experience. It was a spontaneous experience, and a very beneficial one.

Case #3

Use of Psychic Hearing

Several weeks after my experience with Harry was over, I was alone in my office tending to the ever-present paperwork. Harry was no longer in my conscious thoughts.

Someone said, "Sell all your company stock now." It was said softly but with authority.

I looked around to see who had entered my office. No one was there. I shrugged it off, and went back to my work.

"Sell all your company stock now!" This time the voice was louder and closer.

Again, no one was there. I got up and looked into the hallway. No one was there either.

I sat and pondered the words for a few moments. I reasoned that selling the stock was foolish. I had purchased shares of my company's stock through payroll deduction for close to eighteen years. The stock was now worth nearly four-hundred dollars a share and was considered to be the strongest and most valuable stock on the market. Again, I returned to my paperwork.

"Sell all your company stock now!" Now it was a command.

"No!" I mentally retorted.

"I was right about, Harry wasn't I?" the voice boomed.

The hair on the back of my neck bristled. Without hesitation, I picked up the phone and dialed a friend who was a stock broker.

"Don, sell all my stock now."

Don tried for twenty minutes to talk me out of it. It didn't make sense to sell that stock. It was just going to keep going up.

I stuck to my guns, and he finally said, "Okay, Bill, I will place a sell order. But you tell your wife I was against it. I don't want her raising hell with me."

"Now," he continued, "what do you want me to do with the money?"

The voice said, "Reinvest it." So I repeated to Don, "Reinvest it."

"In what?" Don asked.

I paused to wait for the voice to tell me in what, but there was no voice. I felt foolish. I didn't know anything about the stock market.

To keep from appearing to be a complete idiot, I said, "Talk to me about some issues."

Don started talking about issues, but none of it made any sense to me. Then he casually mentioned one issue, which I had never heard of, and the voice said, "Buy that."

"Reinvest all the money in that," I said.

"Bill, you are out of your mind. That is a volatile, high risk issue. You could lose everything in the twinkling of an eye." He spent another twenty minutes trying to dissuade me.

Finally, he relented and placed a buy order. The stock was in South African gold mines.

Epilogue: Two days later the bottom dropped out of the stock I had sold for nearly four hundred dollars a share. It plummeted to one hundred ninety a share in one day. I had sold at a high. It was several years before that stock fully recovered.

A few days after that, the U.S. government lifted the price freeze on gold, and it quickly began to climb. My gold stock soared, split three-for-one, and soared some more.

A little over six months later, while at my desk, the voice said, "Sell." Without hesitation, I sold and made a handsome profit.

Then, unpredictably, I was forced out of the company after eighteen years of service by a series of reorganizations and politics.

My profit from the stock enabled me to live during the next four years while I traveled, studied, became a clinical hypnotist, became a professional astrologer, honed my psychic abilities, engaged in giving psychic readings, and started on the path to becoming a successful author and lecturer. Thus, my life was totally redirected by higher mind. Every step of the way since then I have had psychic guidance and have had the most incredible experiences. In this book, I share a few of these experiences with you to help you learn, but this book is only the tip of the iceberg.

I have no idea how to develop the ability to hear voices, and I wouldn't tell you even if I did know how (I'll explain shortly). I believe, however, that genuine clairaudience is rare and is always spontaneous.

There are certain mental disorders that cause people to hear voices. These are not clairaudience. It may be very difficult to tell the difference, which is why I wouldn't teach how to do it even if I knew how.

A rule of thumb — if you hear voices that tell you to do destructive things, they represent a mental aberration and not clairaudience. Never kill or harm any person or creature because a voice told you to do it. Genuine clairaudience will always provide valuable information that is not harmful to anyone.

The external voice that directed me to sell my stock and reinvest the money in African gold mines was no human being talking to me. It was a voice from somewhere in cosmic consciousness, and I literally heard it just as though it was a physical person standing next to me talking.

Hearing can be an effective psychic tool, although I don't think it is one that occurs very often. However, you do need to sensitize your hearing, and here are some suggestions how.

Exercise #3

Sensitizing Your Sense of Hearing

- When you go to bed at night, lay quietly for a couple of minutes. In bed we usually tune out all sound, unless it is so loud and obnoxious that we are forced to hear it. Instead, concentrate on all of the sounds you hear, and try to identify them.

- Listen carefully. You might hear the refrigerator cycle, or the ice maker drop a load of ice.
- Perhaps a motor vehicle passes on the street; is it a car, a truck, a motor bike?
- Maybe you can hear an airplane; is it a jet, a helicopter, propeller driven?
- Some voices may drift in from outside; are they adult voices or children's voices?

  You get the idea. Identify the sounds of the night whatever they may be, including the sound of your own breathing and heartbeat, or the sounds of your partner (if any). Don't overlook anything. Train your hearing to be sensitive to all sounds, especially the soft sounds that may be almost hidden by other louder sounds. When the psychic mind speaks to you, it is often soft and might be drowned out if you are not sensitive to distinguishing all sounds.
- In the morning, spend a few minutes listening in a similar fashion. Sensitize yourself for the sounds of morning.
- Do you hear a newspaper being delivered, the hum of traffic, birds chirping, a distant siren?
- During the day, listen for the sounds of your environment: a television or radio playing somewhere, a ringing telephone, a distant train, a barking dog.
- Be aware of all sounds, wherever you are.

Once you have practiced this exercise a few times and have sensitized your hearing ability, you will find that external noises will not distract you, unless you need to be aware of a certain noise for your benefit.

If we were always consciously aware of every sound we would probably go crazy. We need to be able to tune out sounds we don't need to hear so that we can maintain our sanity and concentrate on what we are doing, but we need to remain subconsciously aware of all sounds so that when an important sound occurs our subconscious mind alerts us to it.

In Case #3 I described how I was concentrating on paperwork in my office when my subconscious mind alerted me to the psychic voice that told me to sell my stock and reinvest the money.

To assure that you will hear sounds only when it is important, program your subconscious mind.

Here is a sample program to give you the idea. You may alter the program to suit yourself.

Begin by lying in bed with your eyes closed while you listen for the sounds of the night.

- Say to yourself (I always talk out loud to myself unless it is more prudent to talk mentally to myself), "I am now listening to the sounds of the night."
- "The sounds I hear are (name the sounds you hear: a passing motorcycle, your mate snoring, etc.)."
- "I am listening to and identifying these sounds to sensitize my hearing so I may be a more effective psychic practitioner."
- "I command my subconscious mind to always alert me to any sounds that I need to hear for my safety or benefit and for improving my psychic communication with all intelligence in cosmic consciousness."

Use a similar procedure whenever you are sensitizing your hearing.

You don't have to speak out loud if you don't want to. In fact, there are times when it would be prudent to speak only mentally; for instance, when you are riding on the commuter bus to work.

Whenever possible, close your eyes to perform the brief sensitizing program because it is more powerful, usually, than with your eyes open. In a later chapter you will develop your psychic ability to program your subconscious mind to allow you to alter your consciousness and function psychically with your eyes open. For now I recommend that you close your eyes for all exercises whenever possible.

This does not mean that your programming will not work when you perform it with eyes open. It just means that you may have to practice more frequently with your eyes open to achieve the same result that would occur in a shorter time with your eyes closed. Don't get hung up on this — do your programming the best you can, anyway you can, and it will work.

Most of the instructions I have given you here will also apply to all other programming. In future examples I will not repeat the instructions in such great detail as I have here.

You may create your own programming instructions to suit yourself. The examples I give in this book can be changed to fit your personal needs. Of course you may use my example, as is, if you wish.

One thing you will discover as you progress with your psychic development is that you must be flexible in the methods you use. The more you learn and experience, the more you will find that you can change and simplify the mode of operation you employ for using your psychic sense.

Smelling

In the following case study I relate a psychic experience in which my psychic mind alerted me to a paranormal situation by providing a strong scent of roses to get my attention. I have read of similar experiences, in which a person was alerted by a pungent scent of some sort.

Case #4

Use of Psychic Smelling

In March 1980, the Colorado winter was at its coldest and bleakest, with below freezing temperature and a blanket of snow covering everything.

I got into my automobile to go to my job as a sub-contractor writing technical documents for a manufacturing company.

As I started to back out of my driveway, my car suddenly was filled with a powerful scent of fresh roses. I stopped in disbelief and took repeated deep breaths. There was no doubt, it was the scent of hundreds of roses. But how could this be? There were no roses in my car, or in the snow and cold outside.

Because of all the psychic experiences I had had in previous years, I knew something was happening that I didn't understand. I altered my state of consciousness and asked out loud, "What is this all about?"

Immediately I was given awareness of the answer. It was my late sister-in-law, who had died only two weeks before. She was saying "thanks" to me for using hypnosis to ease her suffering during the final weeks of her life, and she was letting me know that she was okay now. I smiled and said, "I love you," and the scent of roses faded and was gone.

One of the most satisfying uses of psychic ability is to contact deceased loved ones, as happened to me in this instance.

While scent may not be a psychic encounter that occurs often, it still is a valuable psychic information path, and you should spend a little time sensitizing your own olfactory sense.

Exercise #4

Sensitizing Your Sense of Smell

- Take a few seconds to relax and sniff the air wherever you are to discover what odors there may be around you.
- Try this exercise in a restaurant or in your kitchen. Open a few containers of spices such as cinnamon, cumin, or basil and sniff them. Sniff whatever foods you may have in your refrigerator.
- Sniff the air when you are putting gas in your car.
- When you identify odors, mentally tell yourself what you are smelling. Say something like, "I am sensitizing my sense of smell for use in my psychic development and I am currently smelling (name of odor)."

You will probably be surprised to discover just how many subtle as well as pungent odors you encounter every day.

Touching

You are most likely to make psychic use of your sense of touch (a physical feeling on your skin) if you are having an encounter with an entity. You may also have physical skin sensations if you are involved in psychic healing.

In the following case, a sensation of heat in my hands occurred while performing psychic healing.

Case #5
Use of Psychic Touching

Of all my psychic experiences, this one stands out in my mind as the most extraordinary.

At the time, my wife worked part-time as a food demonstrator for food brokers. On one occasion while working, she met a woman (I'll call her Nancy) whose husband had been told by his doctor that day that he had only two months to live. The husband (I'll call him Tom) had an infection in his intestine that was literally poisoning him to death; it was untreatable. The infected section of intestine could be removed by surgery, but Tom's physical condition was so debilitated that the doctor said he would surely die on the operating table. Life-saving surgery would kill him, yet he would die without the surgery. Some choice!

Dee was so moved by Nancy's story that she came home that night and asked, "Bill, why don't you help that man?"

"What can I do? If the doctor says there is no hope, I don't see how I can improve matters."

"I've seen you help people. You have a way of just talking to people and making them feel better. Just call Nancy up and ask her and Tom to come over tonight. I have her number."

Dee handed me a slip of paper with a phone number on it. "I don't know these people," I said. "I don't know what to do."

"Just call. You will think of something to say."

I never could refuse my wife anything, so I called and invited Nancy and Tom over. As an aside, I found out later that my wife had told Nancy that I was going to call and ask them over. That explained why they were ready and appeared at our house less than thirty minutes later.

Tom's physical appearance was appalling. His six-foot frame weighed less than a hundred pounds. There was no fleshiness at all, just pale skin tautly stretched over bone. His eyes looked hollow and dead, and he didn't walk; he just shuffled along on feet too heavy for his emaciated legs to lift. His shoulders drooped. Both arms were a mass of seeping scabs from the dozens of injections he had received. He didn't even have enough healing power to heal the puncture wound from a needle. I could easily see why the doctor said that Tom would die on the operating table. The thought crossed my mind that I had seen healthier looking cadavers.

The four of us settled in the living room to talk. Dee served tea. I had no idea what to do or say. I had a vague notion that maybe I could hypnotize him, but then what?

The hypnosis thought flew right out the window as soon as I started to talk to him. He was sixty-five percent deaf in both ears. When I sat directly in front of him and shouted slowly, he got about every third or fourth word. Now what? I didn't know how to hypnotize someone who couldn't hear me, and I sure couldn't do it by writing notes.

So I did what I always do when I don't know what to do. I leaned back, relaxed, and altered my consciousness into theta. I mentally uttered one word to higher mind — "Help!"

And help came thundering into my conscious awareness instantly. I received total awareness of what I should do. Frankly, what I was told to do didn't make any sense to me at all, but I had learned long ago not to question the instructions I receive from higher mind. I just do it.

I led Tom into an adjacent room and motioned for him to sit down in our recliner chair. On a paper I wrote him a note that said, "Lean the recliner back and relax. Close your eyes and do not open them until I touch your forehead." He complied.

Then I took my hands and placed them on each side of his head without actually touching him, about half an inch away. I slowly began to move my hands downward, scanning his entire body. Almost instantly my hands grew hot, as though immersed in hot water. The longer I scanned, the hotter my hands became; they physically became quite red and puffy. I scanned him with my hands for about ten minutes. Then my hands suddenly cooled off and returned to normal color. I knew I was finished, so I touched his forehead to signal him to open his eyes.

Tom bolted from the chair. "My God, what did you do? I felt on fire, but it didn't hurt. I feel great."

His skin had turned a normal pink. His eyes sparkled. And when we walked back to join our wives, he walked briskly.

The rest of the evening he talked non-stop. When we addressed him in our normal speaking voices, he heard every word.

Dee prepared a snack, which he devoured lustily. His wife said he had not eaten solid food in many days.

Over the next several weeks he improved so much that the doctor said he could now survive surgery. The surgery was successful.

I visited Tom in the hospital after surgery. His arms were still full of seeping scabs. Apparently all his healing power had been directed where it was most needed, and the scabs were untreated.

"Bill, can't you do something about these?" Tom asked me, indicating the scabs.

I repeated the same procedure I had used on him several weeks previously.

The next morning Tom phoned to tell me that all the scabs had fallen off during the night, and he was completely healed where the scabs had been.

He was discharged from the hospital a week earlier than the doctor had anticipated.

For the next several weeks I worked with Tom both in person and on the phone. He had the most negative attitude and poorest self-image of any person I had ever met. I told him this was at the root of his problems. I helped him learn self-hypnosis and trained him to restructure himself mentally. Then I put him on his own, with the advice that he had to assume responsibility for his own life. He could not live through me, and I couldn't be available day and night to live for him. I told him that if he returned to his negativism, he would also return to ill health.

At no time did I charge him a penny, nor did he ever offer payment. I felt, and still do, that this was a responsibility and an opportunity for me to serve and learn. At no time did he ever say, "Thank you." His wife did thank me, though. She said that to her knowledge, Tom had never said "Thank you" in his entire life.

For several years Tom practiced off and on what I had taught him and stayed in reasonably good shape, but eventually he allowed himself to slip back into his old negative thought patterns. He stopped trying to help himself. He made life miserable for himself, his wife, and anyone else he came in contact with.

When I found out, Tom was already at death's door again. This time he had given up; he apparently wanted to die. Nothing could be done. He died, but he had gained nearly five extra years of life and had been given the opportunity to learn and grow spiritually. It is unfortunate that he chose not to learn or grow, but he will get the opportunity again sometime, somewhere.

We all get the opportunity to learn, grow, and experience everything necessary for total self-realization. And we get to do it again, and again, and again, as long as necessary until we get it right.

How much better it is if we do it right the first time. Let's make that choice now, and then act on it so we can get on to bigger and better things.

There are two types of exercises that I recommend to sensitize your sense of touch.

Exercise #5

Sensitizing Your Sense of Touch - Temperature

Frequently, a psychic can detect the presence of an entity by a difference in temperature between one location and another. Usually the area near the entity will be quite noticeably cold.

- Place an ice cube or two in one hand. At the same time, place a warm object in the other hand.
- Close your eyes and observe the difference in temperatures.
- Tell yourself you are sensitizing your body to psychically recognize temperature differences.

The warm object might be a freshly toasted piece of bread or a small potato, heated briefly in the microwave. Be careful not to make the object hot enough to burn your skin.

Use your imagination to come up with other objects to give you the hot-cold contrast.

Exercise #6

Sensitizing Your Sense of Touch - Texture

In this exercise you will touch a variety of substances while mentally telling yourself what you are touching. In addition, say something like, "I am now sensitizing my sense of touch for use in my psychic development."

- Choose any substances that are handy, including: food stuffs in your refrigerator, the siding of your house, the sidewalk, furniture, glassware, and so forth. Use your imagination and resources.
- Concentrate on how each substance feels (rough, smooth, slick, gritty, etc.) and remind yourself that you are sensitizing your sense of touch for psychic purposes.

Tasting

I have read accounts of psychics who have had bitter, sweet, and acrid tastes occur during their psychic practice. I have not yet had that kind of experience happen to me, but it might happen to you.

Exercise #7

Sensitizing Your Sense of Taste

- Pause momentarily while eating or drinking and savor the taste of whatever is in your mouth. Mentally remind yourself what you are tasting and mentally say something like, "I am now tasting (name of food) and am sensitizing my sense of taste for use in my psychic development."

■ ■

Chapter 4

ACHIEVING YOUR BASIC PSYCHIC LEVEL

This chapter contains four mental exercises that will enable you to achieve your basic psychic operating level. From this level you can have a nearly endless list of psychic experiences.

All exercises from this point on are specifically designed to bring out your innate psychic and creative abilities, and to sharpen them so that you can begin to function in the psychic realm of your reality.

First we will deal with visualizing the seven basic colors of the spectrum: Red, Orange, Yellow, Green, Blue, Indigo (a very dark blue), and Violet. I use these colors because each color relates specifically to one of your body's chakra centers. Chakras are special power points in your body; a full explanation is beyond the scope of this book. You may want to read more about chakras sometime in the future, but you don't need to know anything about them to function psychically. Just accept that when you visualize the seven basic colors of the spectrum you automatically cause beneficial things to happen within your body.

Exercise #8

Basic Colors #1

- Sit quietly in a place where you will not be disturbed. If there is a telephone nearby, take it off the hook while doing this visualization exercise. The exercise takes only a couple of minutes, although you can continue longer if you wish.
- Close your eyes.
- Take three deeps breaths to relax.
- Visualize yourself holding seven balloons on separate strings: a red one, an orange one, a yellow one, a green one, a blue one, an indigo (dark blue) one, and a violet one.
- One at a time, release the balloons. Allow each one to float up and out of your mental sight. You can release them in any order you wish.
- When you have released them all, open your eyes. Repeat this exercise as often as you wish.

If you have difficulty creating color, do not fret about it. Label the balloons with the words red, orange, yellow, and so forth, and tell yourself these are the colors.

If you have difficulty visualizing at all, just pretend that you have the balloons. Tell yourself the colors and name each one to yourself as you release it.

For all future exercises, if you have difficulty visualizing, follow the example I have described in the two preceding paragraphs, using the details from the new exercise — just pretend. Eventually, you will begin to visualize; for some people, it takes a while to learn how.

The next exercise is a bit more challenging.

Exercise #9

Basic Colors #2

- Close your eyes.
- Allow a red ball to appear at the right side of your mental vision. Allow it to move across your vision and disappear out the left side of your mental vision.
- Then do the same with an orange ball. Continue with all the colored balls of the spectrum.
- Next, bring them back in reverse order from the left side of your vision, across your vision, and out the right side.

These first two exercises are quite important. You learned to:

1. create the seven basic colors,
2. create shapes (balloon shape and ball shape),
3. create and control movement up and across, and
4. relax in a fast and simple manner, allowing your brain to create the alpha waves necessary for good creative visualization.

This next exercise teaches you a simple, but deeper relaxation method that generates strong alpha waves and even theta waves for good psychic performance.

Exercise #10

Deeper Relaxation

- Sit quietly in a place where you will not be disturbed. If there is a telephone nearby, take it off the hook.
- Close your eyes and visualize the sun resting on top of your head. Visualize the number 3 in the center of the sun.

- Allow the sun to move downward through your body, warming and relaxing your body as it goes.
- Feel the warmth and relaxation.
- When the sun reaches your toes, allow it to leave them.
- Then visualize another sun, with the number 2 in it, resting on the top of your head.
- Allow sun number 2 to move downward through your body and exit through your toes, just as sun number 3 did.
- Feel the warmth and relaxation.
- Then visualize another sun, with the number 1 in its center, resting on the top of your head.
- Allow sun number 1 to move downward through your body and exit your toes just as the other two suns did.
- Feel the total relaxation now.
- Say to yourself, "From now on all I need to do to reach this relaxed psychic level is to close my eyes and mentally count from three down to one.
- Open your eyes.

In this session you achieved several important things.

You programmed your mind so that whenever you close your eyes and count down from three to one you will reach a satisfactory psychic level.

You also experienced visualization along with feeling (warmth and relaxation).

You are now learning mechanisms for programming your mind — visualization along with instructions for your subconscious mind.

Now you will learn to go to an even deeper, more effective psychic level. You will achieve this level quickly (almost instantly) with your eyes either open or closed.

This will enable you to be a more effective psychic.

The visualization required is a bit more complex than you have attempted up to this point, but you need to be able to handle complex mental activity if you want to develop your psychic ability.

Read this exercise several times before performing it, just to be sure you understand it and have it fixed in your mind.

Exercise #11

Achieving Your Basic Psychic Level

- Relax in a quiet place, as in the pervious exercises.
- Close your eyes.
- Visualize a spiral staircase with ten steps curving down to the bottom floor.
- Visualize yourself standing at the top of the staircase.
- Take a step down to the ninth step and mentally say "deeper psychic level."
- Then step down to the eighth step and mentally say "deeper psychic level."
- Continue descending the steps as just described.
- When you reach the bottom step, mentally say "I am now at a strong psychic level that I can use for successful psychic performance. I can reach this level whenever I wish, with my eyes either closed or open, simply by desiring to be here and counting from three down to one."
- Open your eyes.
- Next, repeat the above exercise with your eyes open. I recommend that you repeat this exercise at least once a week for a month.

You have now learned to reach a powerful psychic level simply by desiring to do so and counting from three down to one. This only takes about two seconds. When I do it, the image of the staircase always flashes in my mind, reinforcing the exercise. You might want to allow the staircase to flash in your mind when you do the 3-2-1 countdown.

In future exercises I will simply tell you to go to your basic psychic level, and you will do so with the 3-2-1 countdown you learned in this lesson.

We will call this your basic psychic functioning level. Later you will learn an even more profound psychic level, but to reach it you will always begin by going to your basic level.

Nearly all of your psychic practice can be performed at your basic psychic level. Deeper psychic levels are often needed for special psychic functioning, such as past life regression, future progression, or deeper communion with cosmic consciousness. You will learn about these in a later chapter.

All of the case studies in this book were performed at my basic psychic level, unless I specify otherwise.

Every day you will encounter literally dozens of opportunities to use your basic psychic level in small, practical ways to help yourself or others.

Here is just one example.

Case #6 ────────────────────────────
Career Path Change

My youngest daughter, Eileen, was in her final year of high school and planned to go to college. All of her high school courses were business courses, and she had a part time job as a secretary/bookkeeper. For several years, her announced plan was to get a degree in business administration.

One day she seemed troubled and confused. I asked what the problem was. She said she didn't know.

"Then let's find out," I said. I sat down crossed-legged on the floor right then and there, and went to my basic psychic level, where I performed a psychic reading on her.

The information came to me quickly.

"You really don't want a business career," I said. "You recognize it as a good bread-and-butter occupation, but you find it empty of fulfillment and challenge."

"That's true," she responded.

"Your strongest innate asset is your ability to teach children, especially very young children, and you have a great love of children."

"I've never thought about that," she said. "I don't think teaching appeals to me, but I do like the stimulation of small children."

"I am just telling you what your natural abilities are as I read them. Think about it, but don't do it just because I say so. Make your own choice in your own time."

Then I opened my eyes and came out of my basic level. The psychic reading was over.

Eileen started reading literature about teaching and talking to teachers about teaching as a career. Something deep inside her caught fire, and she became excited.

She got her degree in early childhood education and is certified to teach the "little ones," pre-school, kindergarten, and grades one, two, and three. She is delighted with her career choice.

As you become a practicing psychic, look for these little daily opportunities to use your abilities. You will do yourself, others, and the world a lot of good, and you will keep your skills tuned-up. If you want to become a virtuoso in the use of your mind, you must use it as often as you can. "Practice makes perfect" should become your guiding creed.

Right about now you are probably asking, "How do you do a psychic reading?"

All I do is go to my psychic level and visualize the person in my mind. Then I mentally ask questions such as, "What is troubling you?" "How do you feel?" "Tell me about yourself" or whatever questions are appropriate to the situation.

In short, I ask the kind of questions a detective might ask to find information. I am asking at a psychic level and am receiving information directly from the person's psychic mind. This way I receive information that the person may not be consciously aware of knowing.

Recall that all minds are part of cosmic consciousness. That is what makes psychic reading possible.

Sometimes the information I receive is visual. Sometimes I just get a feeling, sometimes I get silent words that flood into my mind, and sometimes I receive mental impressions which I have to translate or interpret. Usually I interpret impressions simply by asking my mind "What does this mean?" I then receive a clearer understanding.

You, too, will eventually experience these things in your own way. It just takes a little time, some patience, and a lot of practice.

■ ■

Chapter 5

PSYCHIC SHIELD

We are all governed by Universal Law. One of these laws is called "The Law of Being."

According to the Law of Being, whatever comes to you, whatever happens to you, whatever surrounds you, will be in accordance with your consciousness and nothing else; whatever is in your consciousness must happen, no matter who tries to stop it; and whatever is not in your consciousness cannot possibly happen.

This simply means that whatever is programmed into your mind will create your reality, and nothing can happen for you or to you if it is not programmed into your mind.

Therefore it makes a lot of sense for you to program yourself with good, beneficial goals and thoughts.

Since our minds can also be programmed by external sources if we do nothing to prevent it, it makes sense for us to take steps to shield ourselves as much as possible from unwanted programming from external sources.

Some external source programming of our minds is beneficial for us and we don't want to eliminate what is good. For example, your guardian angel trying to warn you of a danger is a good external source.

With the preceding statements in mind, you will now program your mind with a psychic shield to exclude all negative or harmful programming from external sources.

In the non-physical world (the psychic world) like attracts like. That is, positive energies attract other positive energies and negative energies attract other negative energies.

You receive negative energies from external sources if you have created negative energies within yourself, allowing other negative energies to be attracted to you.

The solution is to create a powerful shield of positive light that will attract only positive energies and will repel all negative energies. We will also program an awareness into your mind so that when you create negative energy you can immediately cancel it, preventing it from going out into the universe where it might do harm. By being aware of and cancelling any negative energy you create, it will not produce negative karma for you to have to deal with, either in this current lifetime or in a subsequent lifetime.

In the next chapter we will discuss negative energies, demons, and lower astral planes in more detail. Your psychic shield will help you in all of these situations. Because a psychic shield is so important, I want you to create yours now, even though you don't yet know all the reasons for it. Now that you know how to go to your basic psychic level, you need protection.

Exercise #12

Creating Your Psychic Shield

- Sit in a comfortable, quiet place. Take the phone off the hook.
- With your eyes closed, go to your basic psychic level.
- Allow your body to appear in your mental awareness.

- Create a bright, powerful, positive light and allow it to completely envelop your body.
- Say to yourself, "This powerful, positive light is my protective psychic shield."
- "This light will repel all negative energies from programming my mind."
- "This light will allow only positive energies to program my mind."
- "This protective psychic shield will be with me always, from now on."
- "From now on I will be keenly aware of all negative thoughts I may have."
- "I will cancel my negative thoughts by mentally or verbally saying 'NO! I do not want this thought'. The energy from the negative thought will be cancelled by a balancing positive energy."
- Open your eyes.

I recommend that you go to your basic psychic level and call your body with its psychic shield to your mental awareness the day after you do this programming. If your body appears along with the shield of light, say "This is what I want. Thank you." Open your eyes. You should not have to reprogram your shield again unless you have destroyed it by a habitual pattern of negative thinking.

However, if the shield does not appear when you call your body into your awareness, repeat Exercise #12 to create the shield.

Once your body and shield appear when you call them into your mental awareness, you no longer have to reprogram the shield. Reprogram only if the shield does not appear along with your body.

Get in the habit of always saying "No" to yourself whenever you create a negative thought, and immediately force yourself to think some positive thought.

A good way to force a positive thought is to memorize a favorite positive quotation for your use. Select such a quotation and have it handy in your mind to cancel out negative thought patterns.

"Every day in every way I am getting better and better" is a good quotation to use to cancel out negative thought.

I have a number of favorite quotations that I repeat to myself every day just to keep myself tuned up and in a positive frame of mind. You might want to do the same.

Here is a case where a young man almost destroyed himself because he unknowingly allowed himself to be negatively programmed by outside influences. I was able to help him because my psychic shield prevented me from being affected by the powerful negative forces that emanated from and through him.

Case #7

Possessed by the Devil

About ten o'clock one night, my phone rang. A very distraught man was on the other end of the line.

"You don't know me," he said, "but I have heard about you, and I need your help. I am going out of my mind and may kill myself, but I don't want to." He had what I thought might be an Asian accent. My wife is Chinese, and even though she does not have an accent some of her family members do, so I am a little familiar with it.

"What is your name?" I asked.

"Johnny Kim."

"Where do you live?"

He gave me an address in one of the toughest, most undesirable parts of town.

We talked a while, and I became convinced that he did indeed have a serious problem, and that I might be able to help.

I told him I would be there in about a half hour.

"You are crazy!" my wife said. "That part of town isn't safe in daylight, let alone at this time of night. You might be robbed or killed. You don't know that man. You don't owe him anything. If you are killed, what about me? You owe more to me than to some strange voice on the telephone."

I understood her concern and fears, but I also understand the nature of life and of being involved. There is no such thing as not wanting to be involved. We are all born involved whether we want to be or not. Many people choose to ignore that responsibility. I do not choose to ignore it. Also, I have great respect for all races and cultures, and members of many of them have a tough time, so I wanted to help if I could. But this was not the time to discuss the matter with her.

I clipped on my belt holster and slipped my .38 Smith & Wesson revolver into it. Carrying my gun was a precaution for my wife's sake, a show to ally her concerns. I wasn't concerned because I had complete faith in my psychic shield.

"I will be fine, Hon. Please don't worry. I know what I am doing."

Then I left to keep my appointment.

Kim's apartment was what once must have been the attic of a three-story house built around the turn of the century.

He ushered me into his main living area. It was room approximately twenty by twenty feet in size. Except for an old rocking chair in the center, the room was completely devoid of furniture. His wife sat in the chair rocking their infant child; both looked malnourished. A single, unshaded, low wattage light bulb hung from the ceiling. She just nodded and smiled weakly when I said hello. Two blanket pallets that served as their beds occupied a far corner. Some cardboard boxes lined one wall. I assume their few clothes and possessions were in the boxes.

A homemade partition partially separated the kitchen area from the living area, but I could see it quite clearly. It, too, had a single, unshaded low wattage light bulb suspended from the ceiling. Their table was a dilapidated folding card table; next to it were two straightbacked kitchen chairs that appeared to have come from a salvage sale. The stove was a two-burner hot plate. A vintage sink and a homemade cabinet rounded out the appointments. I didn't see a refrigerator.

I assume they had a toilet, but I don't know where it was.

Kim lighted a kerosene lamp and led me into an adjoining space not much larger than a walk-in closet where we were to consult. He set the lamp on the floor. There was not one article of any kind in the room. He fetched the two kitchen chairs for us to sit on.

Then began a strange case. Speaking slowly to make sure I understood him, Kim poured out the essentials of his plight. It seems he worked as a parking lot attendant. His wage was much less than the legal minimum, but he didn't know that. He would have been eligible for welfare which would have paid him more money, but his pride would not permit him to apply for welfare as long as he was capable of working. Desperate for money to provide food and bare survival necessities for his wife and child, he began skimming money from the daily receipts at the parking lot.

He only took what he absolutely needed, and in the week he had been doing it had only skimmed fifty dollars. But he was a very moral person, and his conscience troubled him greatly. He saw himself becoming an habitual thief. He worried about getting caught and being sent to jail. Then what would his wife and child do? If he didn't continue to steal, how could he feed and care for his family?

These things were tearing him up inside, until he was nearly crazy with fear and discouragement. He felt he needed to consult with someone. Kim was not religious, but he believed that talking to a clergyman might help him. Ordinarily this would have been a wise choice, and he would have gotten help. Unfortunately, Kim went to the nearest clergyman who happened to be out of balance himself. The clergyman ranted and raved at Kim, calling him sinful and evil. He said that Kim was damned to hell now and always, that he was possessed of the devil, and that there was no hope for him.

Kim returned home so emotionally shaken that he was planning to kill himself. He was absolutely convinced he was possessed of evil. Only the sight of his wife and child, whom he loved, made him determined to look elsewhere for help. He recalled seeing a small ad I had placed in the personal column of a newspaper he borrowed from someone, and he phoned me.

Clearly, there were two things I needed to do. First, rid Kim of his fear, and second, help him get financial support.

I altered my state of consciousness to my basic psychic level and did a psychic reading. I immediately encountered a powerful negative wall of fear that was difficult to penetrate. So I directed my attention to the clergyman and told Kim what I found. In essence, the clergyman was an old man who was bitter about being sent to this rundown parish to spend his final years. He felt he deserved better recognition from his church. He also was somewhat mentally out of balance, due partly to his failing health and partly to his negative attitude. He was an old school traditionalist who saw everything as either black or white, and he saw evil everywhere. He also had a considerable amount of racial prejudice.

I sent the clergyman love, courage, and peace. Then I redirected my attention to Kim.

After hearing what I could tell him of the clergyman, Kim's wall of fear was considerably less powerful, and I was able to establish solid contact at a psychic level with him.

It was quickly apparent to me that he was a good person, trying to do his best, but he didn't know how to go about it. He was very naive, uneducated, and socially unsophisticated. Higher mind also told me that Kim really did believe that he was possessed of evil.

In reality, he was not possessed at all, but he really believed he was. So higher mind directed me to exorcise the evil from him so he would feel balanced and clean again.

I didn't know anything about exorcism, but higher mind directed me through the procedure.

I am not putting the exorcism procedure I used in this book. This sort of thing can potentially get you into a lot of trouble; it also can be dangerous in some circumstances. It is not something you are likely to ever need, and I don't want you experimenting with it. If you ever need to know about exorcism, I will leave it up to your own experience and your higher mind to direct you.

After the exorcism, Kim felt fine. He knew that there was nothing wrong with him now.

Then I hypnotized Kim and directed him through imagery and suggestions to create a good self-image of himself.

After that, I talked to him about applying for food stamps and looking into welfare. I wrote down the names of the agencies he needed to contact. I had convinced him that there was no shame in asking for help; that was what the agencies were for. He said he would contact the welfare people in the morning.

Because he was still bothered about the theft of money, I outlined a plan for him to follow. He was not to tell anyone about the theft because they wouldn't understand. Instead, he was to take four dollars a day out of his wages and slip it into the day's receipts until he had replaced all he had taken. He said he would do this, and it was apparent that he felt good about himself and the future.

Then I went home satisfied that higher mind, channeled through me, had enriched another life.

■ ■

Chapter 6

Becoming a Psychic

You have now learned how to achieve your basic psychic level, from which you can have an endless number of psychic experiences as a practicing psychic. As you develop and sharpen this skill, there is virtually no limit as to what you can experience and do.

Becoming a practicing psychic is a serious commitment. It will not work unless you enter into it with integrity, dedication, and a sincere desire to enrich yourself and all with whom you interact.

All the exercises in this book are carefully structured to awaken and sharpen your innate psychic abilities. Since no two people are alike, there are no guarantees as to precisely what each individual will achieve from these exercises.

Before we go into additional exercises there are some things you need to know about the psychic world.

The Psychic World

As a psychic practitioner, you will sometimes encounter experiences that are quite startling. Once you have gained some experience, you will easily handle whatever occurs without any undue concern, but in the beginning phases of your learning, some experiences can be quite upsetting. I want to alert you to this because you may well encounter some unusual experiences, and I don't want you to let it frighten you and prevent you from continuing to pursue your psychic development. Here is one such experience I had.

Case #8
Terminally-Ill Child

In February 1972 I was still in the beginning stage of performing as a practicing psychic. A man came to me and asked me to tune in to his eight-year-old niece, who lived in another state. I was not emotionally prepared for what happened.

I altered my consciousness to my basic psychic level and invoked the image of the little girl in my mental vision. She appeared, and within seconds I watched her wither up and die. Then I saw a casket with a calendar on top of it. The calendar said May 2, 1972. I began to weep profusely over the death of this beautiful child. I was emotionally shaken to the bones. NOTE: I must have been in the theta range of brain frequency because that is where our emotions are recorded.

I remained in theta and psychically examined the child; I discovered that she had leukemia. I then attempted to perform psychic healing for her benefit. I say "attempted" because I was stopped almost immediately by a command from higher mind not to interfere in this case. The death was necessary for reasons that did not concern me. This caused me to weep uncontrollably. My face was wet, and I could feel the tears dripping onto my chest and lap.

Remaining in theta, I then directed love, courage, and peace to the child by speaking out loud while keeping her image in my mental vision. I said something like, "I love you and God loves you, and He sends you courage and peace using me as his instrument." When I felt that she had indeed received and accepted the love, courage, and peace I brought myself out of theta and opened my eyes. I was still crying. It was a minute or so before I gained control of my emotions and could speak.

Her uncle's face was ashen. He knew from my visible reaction that something was wrong. I told him everything. He then told me he had feared something was wrong, and that was why he had come to me. It seems he had visited his brother and sister-in-law and their child the previous week. The child had become sickly, but the parents refused to take her to a doctor. He said his brother and sister-in-law were miserly cheap, even though they were financially sound. They weren't going to "throw good money to a doctor when all that was wrong was a little head cold."

I advised him to get the child to a doctor immediately. He said he was going to fly back to Texas in the morning and personally take the child to a doctor and pay the bill himself.

Several weeks later, the uncle contacted me and confirmed that he had done just as he had vowed. The parents let him take the child for medical attention as long as he agreed to pay all expenses. The prognosis was grim. The child had terminal leukemia.

In May, the uncle again contacted me to let me know the child had died on May 2.

There are several things to learn from this case history.

1. You may very well encounter experiences that will shake you up. Through experience and sufficient pre-conditioning of yourself, you will learn to handle anything. So do not let these experiences deter you from practicing and progressing.

2. You are not always able to help in the manner you would like to. I was thwarted from performing psychic healing by a higher power that had a more complete understanding of the case than I did.

3. You can always send love, courage, and peace to anyone, any place, any time without restriction, and this includes drawing in generous portions of love, courage, and peace to yourself from cosmic consciousness. I heartily recommend you develop the daily habit of sending these energies to others and to yourself.

4. Sometimes you experience things exactly as they are, and sometimes you experience symbols of an event that provide a shorthand version of a situation. In this instance, I had both elements. The quick withering away was a shorthand version of what would happen over the next several months. The casket symbolized death. The calendar reflected exactly the time of death.

You have to be careful in interpreting symbols. In this case, I correctly interpreted the casket as meaning physical death. Several years later, while doing a projection forward in time, I encountered a person and a casket. Again, I interpreted this as the physical death of that person. I was wrong. What actually occurred was the death of that person's profound negativism and self-destructive thought patterns. Had I been more careful and thorough in my psychic investigation of that person I would have discovered the truth. Instead I jumped to a conclusion because a casket had once been correctly indicative of physical death. I learned a valuable lesson. Fortunately, I had not told anyone about the "death" so no harm was done.

So learn from my mistake — be cautious, and thorough, and always be very discrete about pronouncing a verdict of death. I have since adopted a rule to never mention physical death when I see it unless there are some exceptionally compelling reasons to do so. So far, I have not encountered sufficiently compelling reasons.

Another kind of unexpected encounter that I want to caution you about is one that can be terrifying.

Sometimes when you enter the psychic world you inadvertently enter one of the lower astral planes, inhabited by extremely negative energies.

For most people no harm can come of these encounters other than having the daylights scared out of you. There is a way to handle these encounters.

I put this exercise in at this point because it fits in with the discussion. I hope this is one exercise you will never have to use, but read it, just in case.

Exercise #13

Getting Rid of Demons and Other Unwanted Energies

- You will most likely already be at your basic psychic level when you encounter a demon or other negative entity.
- If not, enter your basic psychic level.
- Point your finger and then snap your fingers at the energy (demon if you prefer) that is threatening to you.
- Each time you point and snap, say "shrink" and the energy will shrink fifty percent.
- Continue to rapidly point and snap and say "shrink," point and snap and say "shrink," until the energy just disappears.

As an aside, this is an excellent exercise to teach children to rid them of their nightmares. Children are already at a basic psychic level most of the time, so there is no need to teach them how to achieve it. A child's brain frequency is predominantly in the alpha range; that is why children learn so rapidly and so well.

I said "most" people cannot be harmed in these encounters. That means some can be. The danger is that one of these energies could enter and possess your body. There are only four ways this can happen:

1. You are out of control due to alcohol or drugs.
2. Through ignorance, you actually invite the energy to enter.
3. Through fear, you are intimidated into inviting the energy to enter.
4. You have a defect in your aura due to some grave personality defect such as schizophrenia.

Item #1 is easily handled. Do not use drugs or excessive alcohol. If you are under the influence of alcohol or drugs, that does not mean you will become possessed. It means that the risk is there, and it could happen. It is not worth the risk.

Item #2 is being handled by your reading this book and becoming informed. You know that the energy cannot enter you unless you actually invite it in, so don't make the invitation. It is that simple.

Item #3 is also handled by this book if you complete the exercises I have provided. The protective psychic shield you created in the last chapter will help a great deal to repel external negative energies. Exercise #13, which we just finished, gives you a method for getting rid of the demon. Again, don't invite the unwanted energies in. You are in control, and no one or no thing has the right to intimidate you. You will not be intimidated unless you willingly allow it.

I am not able to help you with Item #4. People in this category are in much more danger of possession than those in all other groups combined, and I don't know how to prevent it except to say that if you have some grave personality disorder, do not practice psychic excursions.

Let's continue discussing negative energy, but from a different perspective.

Every person in the world is an energy source. That means both positive and negative energy. The negative energies from other people cannot harm you unless you allow it. Your protective psychic shield will help against outside harm.

Of greater concern is the negative energy you generate. If you generate negative energy, it will, like the proverbial chickens, come home to roost. You cannot protect yourself from your own negative energy. You created it, you own it, and sooner or later you must deal with it in some fashion.

Before you panic, let me say that there are effective ways to counteract the negative energy that you generate so that you do not have to bear the full brunt of its return.

In essence, you override the negative with massive positive energy.

A simplistic example: You speak unjustly about a person and cause him problems (you created a negative energy karma) and thus create the need for a counterbalancing positive energy (karma). If you do nothing, the negative karma will return to you in some manner — perhaps you will be unjustly lied about, perhaps something else will occur. The Law of Ten-Fold applies to negative karma as well as to positive karma, so you could well receive ten times the return. However, this does not have to be. You can avert the negative karma by creating overriding positive karma. In this example, you might take the following steps:

1. Alter your state of consciousness.
2. Forgive yourself and ask forgiveness of the person you wronged. Ask through higher mind, which embraces both of you.
3. Send love, courage, and peace to the person you wronged.
4. Correct the situation completely for the wronged person. Visualize him with his reputation restored, receiving increased respect from others, and so forth.
5. Program yourself again to become immediately aware when you are about to create negative energy so that you can immediately stop it through that awareness. Ask higher mind to empower you to control yourself better.

You will want to repeat steps 1, 2, and 3 over a several day period, depending on the severity of the situation you caused. Once is sufficient for minor infractions.

Of course, if there is something physical that needs balancing, you should do that also. For example, if you stole a neighbor's tool box, either return it or send an appropriate amount of money anonymously in the mail. This is in addition to the psychic steps listed above.

By using your positive energy you can minimize, and sometimes eliminate, the need to experience a negative counterbalancing as a result of your ill-advised negative action.

ONE CAUTION: Do not use this avenue of balancing as a way of doing whatever you want (negatively) and then escaping the consequences. Such behavior brings with it dire consequences. Your psychic ability is a precious gift, and deliberate continued misuse of it brings a karma that cannot be avoided but must be experienced. Psychic ability must be used with a sense of responsibility and integrity. If not, you will have to learn your lesson through a very difficult route. Do not let that happen to you. Remember, you always have a choice. Choose wisely.

Concept of Psychic Development

At this point, you should have a fairly good idea of what the psychic world is about and what you have to do to enter the psychic world. As a refresher, here are salient points:

1. Thought is an energy that cannot be destroyed, and thought creates everything. You will learn to use thought to create results you want and to communicate with cosmic consciousness.
2. To invoke your psychic mind, you need to alter your state of consciousness (that is, slow down your brain frequency).
3. Hans Berger discovered that you can slow your brain frequency simply by closing your eyes.
4. Further experimentation reveals that mental visualization greatly enhances psychic ability.
5. Everyone has some innate psychic ability.
6. Everything that has ever happened or will happen is recorded somewhere in cosmic consciousness.

Simply put: If you slow down your brain frequency by closing your eyes, you can use your mind and visualization abilities to function as a practicing psychic.

Of course, there is a bit more to it than just closing your eyes. You have to condition your senses and your mind to do what you want. You do this by repetitious mental exercises until your mind understands that you really want to develop and use all your psychic facilities; then your mind makes it happen, and you start functioning as a psychic.

For some of you this will happen fairly quickly. For others it will take a little longer. The secret is persistence and determination in practicing mental exercises to condition your mind.

You have a built-in mechanism for conditioning your mind to function psychically. That mechanism is called your subconscious mind. In Chapter 1, I gave you a brief definition of the subconscious mind and said I would discuss this later in the book. Now is the time for that discussion.

Your subconscious mind has some very special properties. The alpha range of brain activity is considered to be the area in which your subconscious mind operates. Remember, when you close your eyes your brain begins generating strong waves of alpha, which means that you have excellent access to your subconscious mind when your eyes are closed.

The subconscious mind does not think, does not rationalize or reason, does not know good from bad, does not know right from wrong. The subconscious mind just does what it is told to do. Like an obedient servant, it just follows orders without ever questioning anything.

If you were to tell yourself often enough that you were a stupid, clumsy idiot, your subconscious mind would interpret that as an order to be carried out, and you would begin to behave in a stupid, clumsy, idiotic manner.

Conversely, if you told yourself often enough that you were capable of being a good psychic and that is what you wanted, your subconscious mind would interpret that as an order, and you would begin to function as a psychic.

As an aside, you can readily see how words can have an impact on people. For example, a child repeatedly chastised by a parent for being no good will grow up to be no good, because whatever the child's subconscious is told, the child's mind makes happen.

To summarize: this psychic development business is all about choice. You program your own psychic mind with information that enables you to function psychically whenever you wish. With your psychic shield you have already programmed your subconscious mind to ignore any programming from other people and to follow only the programming that you personally perform.

The series of simple mental and visual exercises in this book that you can do in minutes (often in seconds) anytime, anywhere, will allow you to accomplish as much as you deserve to accomplish. By deserve, I mean that the more diligently you practice and the more determined and persistent you are, the more you will accomplish.

There is no pressure on you to practice any of the exercises in this book. You can do all of them if you wish. You can select some and not others. It is your choice.

This book is designed to take you to some level of psychic competence if you do all the exercises. When you finish the book, you will probably select a couple of exercises that you especially like to use. Perhaps you will develop exercises of your own based on what you have learned.

There is no one best way that I know of for developing psychic ability. What I offer in this book is simply one way that will work. In my own experimentation I have discovered many ways to enter the psychic realm; some of those ways are deceptively simple once you have already reached some level of psychic performance.

I feel confident that you will also develop your own methods once you start using your psychic ability routinely.

When you boil it all down, becoming a psychic is about solving problems, whether your own or someone else's. All the case studies in this book solved some sort of problem.

Frequently I have mentioned psychically sending love, courage, peace, and help to others. This is done quite simply by going to your psychic level, visualizing what needs to be done, and speaking your intention, either mentally or out loud. To send love to your mother, for example, just mentally visualize her at your psychic level and say, "I love you, Mom, and I channel love from cosmic consciousness to you."

Here is a case where several people combined forces to channel love and help to another person. This is one more example of the things you can do every day as a psychic.

Case #9

Grandson's Eye Surgery

This case illustrates the use of group energy to achieve a desired result.

In 1983 my grandson, Sean, was eight years old. He had to have eye surgery. The usual after-effects from this kind of surgery are a few days of: blood seepage from the eye; swelling in and around the eye; discoloration similar to a black eye;

minor, but nagging discomfort; and perhaps some temporary vision disfunction.

The night before and morning of the surgery, I went to my psychic level and psychically sent Sean love, courage, and peace. I also mentally told him that everything would be fine and he would heal rapidly and completely.

Sean spent the night before his surgery at our house with Dee and I. Our eldest daughter Jeanne, Sean's mother, also stayed with us, so he had the benefit of being in the presence of three loving, positive auras.

Jeanne and Dee are both tuned in to the powerful effects of positive energy. They and I, each in our own ways, sent healing energy, love, and courage to Sean, starting the night before surgery.

All three of us were with Sean prior to, during, and immediately after surgery, constantly sending healing energy to him. I went to my psychic level when Sean returned to his room after surgery and performed psychic healing by visualizing him completely healed, smiling, energetic, and happy, and by mentally removing any damage that I sensed.

The results were spectacular. He had absolutely no swelling or discoloration. There was no bleeding, no discomfort, and no vision problems. There was no visible evidence of his having had surgery.

He didn't even get an upset stomach from the anesthesia. The anesthesia wore off completely in about two hours. He jumped up and said, "I want to go home." He was discharged immediately and we went home, where he began playing as though nothing had ever happened.

The more people you can get to use their psychic energy in concert, the more spectacular the results. The power of combined energies seems to increase by an order of magnitude.

For instance, if one person represents X-power, two persons in combined effort seem to generate X-power squared; three persons in combined effort, X to the fourth power; four persons, X to the eighth power, and so on. Each additional person in a combined effort seems to cause the power factor to double over the previous power factor. It pays to work in concert with others. The possibilities of this are awesome.

If the majority of a particular race of people believe they are somehow inferior to another race, they most assuredly will perform (collectively) in such a manner as to be perceived and treated as inferior by themselves and by others. The few who do not subscribe to the "inferior" belief will stand out, achieve much, and be leaders. If these few leaders ever use their psychic power to persuade the rest of their race that they are not inferior, stand back and watch the powerful results. As the tide of psychic energy swells in a positive direction within that race, things begin to happen not only with them, but within the world. They will shatter the bonds of "inferiority" and assume their rightful and equal place within society. Does this ring a bell? History, including current history, is replete with evidence of this kind of power.

As a person thinks, so he/she is. As groups of people think, so becomes the world.

Are you beginning to see now how you can use your psychic power? Do you see how world peace can be obtained? Do you see how hunger need not be a reality in the world? Do you see how psychic power embraces everything from healing a minor

paper cut to healing the world? From achieving a happy marriage to achieving a happy society? From gaining a promotion in
your work to promoting harmony among all people?

By the end of this book, you should begin to *see,* to get a *feel*
for, to *hear* the sound of, the message of what psychic power is
all about.

If you don't, I suggest you re-read the book. On the first
reading you will have learned how to develop and unleash your
psychic powers. It stands to reason that you ought to acquire
some semblance of insight before using that power.

■ ■

Chapter 7

VISUALIZATION

The exercises in this chapter give you additional opportunities to use your basic psychic level and to develop your visualization faculties. These exercises rely partly on your memory and are partly visualizations about yourself. They are ground breakers for more extensive work yet to come.

Exercise #14

The Chalkboard

- Go to your basic psychic level.
- Visualize a chalkboard such as you had when you attended school. In the chalk tray are an eraser and pieces of chalk
- Pick up a piece of chalk and draw a large circle on the chalkboard.
- Print the initial of your first name inside the circle.
- Now erase the initial from inside the circle without erasing the circle.
- Mentally tell yourself, "I can visualize anything I wish, anytime I wish."
- Now erase the circle and open your eyes.

This exercise enabled you to create something from nothing, then mentally change what you had created. It also provided positive programming of your subconscious mind that you can do this anytime you wish.

Here is a case where I created a repair shop for my motor home to get me and my family out of a dangerous situation.

Case #10 ————————————————————
Motor Home Repair

My wife, our youngest daughter and her dog, and I were returning from a day's outing in the Rocky Mountains in our motor home. It was late in the evening and quite dark. We were twenty miles from the next town. I was driving up a steep mountain road when the engine died. My efforts to restart the engine were unsuccessful. I couldn't just stay there because of the obvious hazard, and I couldn't let the motor home roll backward down the twisting mountain road in the dark; that would be suicide. The only viable solution was to repair whatever was wrong, then start the engine and drive out of there. I didn't have the luxury of much time to do it in. To make matters worse, I know next to nothing about vehicles other than how to drive them. My wife was becoming extremely upset. So was the dog. I had to do something.

I asked my wife and daughter to be quiet for just a few minutes. I closed my eyes and altered my state of consciousness. I brought my motor home into my mental vision along with a group of expert mechanics. I told the mechanics to fix the engine well enough to get us to the next town safely. I gave them two minutes, visualizing the group of expert mechanics changing parts and quickly putting everything in the engine compartment into proper operating condition.

Then I opened my eyes and turned the key in the ignition. The engine started immediately, and I drove to the next town. As I pulled into a service station the engine promptly died.

The service station was just closing. When I explained my problem the mechanic took a brief look at the motor home. He couldn't start it. He gave me permission to camp overnight in front of his gas station until the next day when the problem could be investigated more thoroughly.

The next day the mechanic found the problem. The starter motor was completely shot. Whatever was inside the starter motor was ground to bits. The mechanic poured ground metal from it. He showed me what was left of the starter. "This kind of damage couldn't occur in just a short time," he said. "There is no way you could possibly have started your engine with this starter motor.

I told him about how I started it and where I had driven from the night before.

"That just is not possible," he said.

There will be times in your life when you will need to do the "impossible" just as I did that dark night on the side of the mountain. Use your psychic ability to do it.

Exercise #15

Sky Writing

- Go to your basic psychic level.
- Visualize an airplane in the sky.
- The airplane is leaving a trail of fluffy white vapor.
- Allow the airplane to write your first name with the vapor trail in the sky.

- See your first name in white, fluffy letters in the sky.
- Now let the wind blow your name away, carrying it into the universe where you are functioning as a psychic.
- Mentally tell yourself, "I am becoming a better and better psychic every time I perform visualization."
- Open your eyes.

In this exercise you have reinforced programming in your subconscious that you are a successful psychic.

Exercise #16

Visualizing Your Own Body

- Go to your basic psychic level.
- Cause your own body to appear in your mental imagery. Study your body in detail, front and rear.
- Mentally describe what you are looking at. For example, think, "Long blond hair. Small mole on left cheek. Skinny legs." Be specific.
- Study your body until you are intimately familiar with it in its exterior appearance.
- Mentally say to yourself, "I can bring the presence of any creature into my mental vision merely by asking that creature to appear to me."
- When you are finished, open your eyes.

Some of your future psychic work may be with people or concerning people, and you will often need to call them into your mental imagery to communicate with them.

By having you visualize your own body, I condition you to look at bodies without embarrassment.

You are not invading a person's privacy by calling him or her into your mental vision. What you are really doing is establishing a psychic communications link with that person. The person (or creature or entity) that you call into your mental vision may not necessarily look exactly like a photograph. In fact, the image may be fuzzy or just a suggestion of some person, creature, or entity. You may see only a formless shape. When you call someone or something into your mental vision, whatever image you get is okay, because all you are doing is establishing communications. Recall what I said in an earlier chapter — just pretend; it works.

To help others or to perform psychic healing on people or any other creature, it is most effective when you bring the person's or creature's presence into your mind. Here is how I did this with a dog.

Case #11 _____
Takra

Takra, my youngest daughter's beautiful Samoyed dog, had become seriously ill with a life-threatening anal infection. The veterinarian's best efforts for several weeks had failed to bring about any improvement in Takra's condition.

The doctor finally said that it was too serious a matter to continue to try to treat with medication because the dog was not responding at all. Takra, usually an energetic animal, just lay listlessly and in some discomfort. He wouldn't eat or drink. The doctor said surgery was necessary, and it needed to be performed immediately. He said the dog's chances of surviving surgery were only fifty-fifty.

My daughter said, "No!" She feared the dog would die from the anesthesia. Also she didn't want him cut on. She was hoping for a miracle.

She came to me, sobbing, "Daddy, can't you help Takra? I have seen you help people. Why not a dog?"

"I'll give it my best shot," I promised.

I sat down crosslegged in the middle of the floor, closed my eyes, and altered my consciousness to my basic psychic level.

I mentally commanded the image of Takra to enter my mind. With my intelligence, I scanned his entire body internally and externally, and corrected all the abnormalities I detected. The anal region was a mass of pus, infection, blood, and redness.

When I function psychically, I have everything I need to correct any problem because I mentally create whatever I need. To get rid of the pus, I created a powerful suction tube similar to that used by dentists which I mentally inserted into the area filled with pus. I drew out all the pus. I mentally scraped off all the infection with steel wool and cleansed the area with a powerful medicine labeled "cure all" from my mental medicine chest. I processed all of Takra's blood through a purifying machine and filled him with the cleansed blood. I sprayed the area with a color restorer so that everything looked normal and healthy. Then I took a needle labeled "strength and energy" and gave him an injection. Satisfied that Takra was restored to health and balance, I opened my eyes.

My daughter immediately went to the room where Takra had been lying. She found him standing and stretching as though awakening from a long nap. He pounced at her, wanting to play. She examined him externally. There was no seepage, no swelling, no discoloration. He looked and acted fine.

The next day she took him to the vet where he was given a clean bill of health.

"The medicine must have had a long-delayed action," the vet said. "I've never seen anything like that before, but what else could it have been?"

What else, indeed?

The kinds of things I've described here are things you can do, too. The next chapter will give you a start with an exercise on mentally scanning the inside of your own body.

In psychic healing you symbolically do whatever is natural for you to do to correct the problem.

For instance, you might perceive a defective kidney as having bumps on it. You can sand off the bumps with a power sander and paint the kidney to restore its natural color. You might treat leukemia by having millions of cancer-eating piranha swimming in the bloodstream and devouring the cancer cells. A blocked intestine might be cleared by using a roto-rooter. A damaged nerve could be replaced by a fine, sensitive wire. Your powerful imagination and visualization, exercised at your basic psychic level, make the psychic power work. If you visualize a roto-rooter cleaning out a blockage, your mind and the recipient's mind translate that image into natural healing action.

■ ■

Chapter 8

PSYCHIC HEALING

Being an instrument in psychic healing is without question in my mind the most rewarding and humbling service you can provide as a psychic.

Several of the cases presented thus far have had elements of psychic healing in them.

The way to learn psychic healing is to just do it, and have faith that it will work if success is in the subject's, and your, best interest. You can find hundreds of opportunities every day: You read in the paper that someone has been hurt in an accident; a friend is injured or ill; a family member is in pain or distress; a family pet needs help. Take the time to mentally explore the situation and correct it.

If you are physically present, you can also use the power of your aura and hands (reference Case #5 in Chapter 3).

Always help when asked. If the person is unable to ask, assume they would ask if they could, and offer to help.

The only healing ability that you personally possess is the ability to heal yourself — that is all. You are not the source of healing power for anyone else. All healing comes from the Supreme Source (God) and from the self-healing power vested within each creature by that Supreme Source.

As a psychic healer you are an instrument or catalyst for triggering the innate self-healing ability of the person or creature to whom you direct your energies. You act as a channel through whom God provides healing energy.

This analogy might help put psychic healing into perspective. A lamp has wiring, a light bulb, and a switch. The lamp, therefore, has the innate ability to give light. An electric generator from the public service company many miles away is the source of power for the lamp. However, the lamp will not give light unless the switch is turned on.

Now substitute God for the electric generator, substitute health for the glowing light bulb, and substitute self-healing power for the switch. As a psychic healer, your job is to turn on the switch.

You do it by a mystical process that you will probably never understand. I know I don't understand it.

When I act as a psychic healer, as described in this book, I am merely offering myself as a "go-between" to turn on the switch. I make myself available, and the Supreme Source does the rest.

Unless you are a licensed medical practitioner, do not attempt to give medical advice or to act as though you were a medical practitioner.

Recently my wife was in a life-threatening situation. (Later the doctor told us she was within three hours of death when I brought her to him). When she became stricken, I immediately took her to an excellent physician. I did not sit down and attempt to perform psychic healing. What I did do was send her help via my aura and presence while transporting her to the doctor. Once she was in the hands of the physician, I performed mental psychic healing. Later, in private, I also performed "hands-on" psychic healing. My psychic healing augmented the work of the physician; it did not replace it. She pulled through — a happy ending.

When you realize that you are part of an awesome healing process for someone else, it is a humbling experience. You recognize that you personally do not have that power; furthermore you don't even know exactly what you did. It is a mystical process. Yet it works!

I am personally acquainted with a psychic (ex-psychic would be more accurate) whose ego grew so large that she thought she was a grandiose source of mystical power, personally causing things to happen. At that point she lost all of her ability — one hundred percent of it!

Her ego is still so enormous that she doesn't recognize that she has not, to my knowledge, accomplished even one psychic achievement in over fifteen years. Instead she revels in the tales of her past glories. How sad.

I encourage you to attempt psychic healing at every opportunity, and to do so with the faith and the sense of naive wonderment of a child. Then you will succeed.

When you use your psychic powers to help people who are ill or injured, you will sometimes need to psychically look inside the person to see if you sense any abnormalities or injuries.

When you sense an abnormality or injury you will want to psychically fix it. The process of doing this sends love and healing energy to the person, and also helps to trigger the person's own healing powers.

Remember — DO NOT PLAY DOCTOR! Unless, of course, you are a licensed physician.

Your role in psychic healing is to augment the treatment provided by a physician. NEVER ADVISE A PERSON TO DO SOMETHING AGAINST HIS OR HER DOCTOR'S ADVICE!

Before performing the exercise in this chapter you should have some awareness of what a person's body should contain: blood vessels, muscle, tissue, various organs (heart, liver, etc.), skeletal structure, tendons, nerves, brain, cells, etc. If you do not have much awareness in this area, get a book on anatomy from the library. Study the pictures and read sufficient material to develop some working knowledge of the body.

You might also want to review Case #11 in the preceding chapter to see how I handled the Takra (dog) case. This might stimulate your own creative mind so you will be able to scan the bodies of any creature and fix anything that you sense is not right.

I am not able to tell you specifically what an abnormality looks like because we each psychically perceive abnormalities in a different way. For example, a defective kidney might look bloated to one person, shriveled to another. It might appear full of holes, have hairline cracks, or possess an unhealthy color. You will have to rely on your own intuitive perception in this matter.

How you fix any problems is again an individual choice: replacing the part, patching it up, pouring a cure-all medicine on it. You must use your own creative mind to determine how to handle the situation.

Exercise #17

Psychically Examining Your Own Body

- Go to your basic psychic level.
- Call the presence of your own body into your psychic mental vision. Examine your body internally with your

psychic mind. Look at everything: heart, liver, stomach, intestines, sex organs, kidneys, gall bladder, blood vessels, lungs, nerve system, brain, bone structure, eyes, muscles, and so forth.

- Take your time; do a thorough job.
- Correct abnormalities, if any, when you sense them, using your psychic creativity.
- When you are finished with your examination, say "I am now healthy," and open your eyes.

Case #12 _____
Ask Higher Mind

Once while doing a psychic scanning of another person's body, his image in my mental vision had a right eye that kept twinkling, much as a star in the sky appears to twinkle. This perplexed me, so I asked my higher mind what this twinkling meant. The answer I was given was that the man was blind in his right eye and had an artificial eye installed. I later found out that this was true.

I relate the preceding story to you so you will know that all you need to do during any psychic procedure is to ask higher mind for help when you are perplexed or confused.

When you psychically send help to someone, you don't need to tell them what you are doing. In fact, you often can give more benefit if you don't tell them because they will not then consciously resist your efforts.

You can help strangers. You read in the newspaper that someone is badly burned in an explosion. Psychically project health, healing, freedom from unnecessary pain, courage, faith, love, and other caring thoughts.

All this costs is a few minutes of your time, and it can make a tremendous difference to the one you are helping.

You gain also: first, in knowing that you acted as a loving, responsible citizen of the universe; second, because every time you use your psychic abilities they become stronger and more effective.

Develop the practice of immediately sending help, if only for a second or two, to every person you become aware of who needs help.

■ ■

Chapter 9

CREATING YOUR PSYCHIC GOAL BOWL

You will now have the opportunity to use your basic psychic level to set and achieve goals.*

It is basic human nature to have a simple desire such as "being liked by others." Nor is it unusual to have a major desire such as "learning to walk again after a crippling accident." There are an infinite number of desires that one may have, from the trivial to the most profound.

Some people have great success in achieving most of their desires. Some people have little or no success. Others seem to have some successes and some non-successes.

What makes some people more successful than others in achieving their desires?

The successful people turn their desires into specific goals and then program their higher mind with commands to achieve those goals.

The unsuccessful people merely turn their desires into wishes. If you put all your wishes in one hand, and pile garbage in the other hand, the hand with garbage will fill up much faster.

---

* Most of this chapter has been excerpted from an article I wrote for *FATE* Magazine and is reprinted here by permission of *FATE* and Llewellyn Worldwide, Ltd.

In other words, mere wishes land you in a pile of garbage, not in a pile of achieved goals.

We all have the ability to achieve goals if we know how to go about it. All we have to do is communicate effectively with our higher mind exactly what we expect our mind to achieve for us.

If you think your life is directed by whims of fate over which you have no control, think again. You create your own fate by what you do, or don't do, with your psychic mind.

You can program your higher mind with junk and thus have a junky life. You can refuse to program your higher mind, and then others will program it for you, giving you a life that is not your own but is rather the life of a puppet dancing to everyone else's tune. Or you can choose to take responsibility for yourself and program your psychic mind in a constructive manner so as to achieve some measure of success and happiness for yourself. The choice is yours alone to make. Your fate is up to you.

To choose success and happiness instead of the garbage pile, I will now show you a simple, effective, and somewhat off-beat method of programming your higher mind with beneficial goals.

I call this my "Psychic Goal Bowl" method.

Case #13

Goal Bowl Concept

In the early 1970s I took a cereal bowl from a set of dishes that we were replacing and labeled it "Bill Hewitt's Psychic Goal Bowl." I placed the bowl in the top drawer of the nightstand on my side of the bed.

Whenever I had a goal I wanted to achieve, I would write the goal on a small piece of paper and write the date. Sitting in bed before turning out the light to sleep, I would read the goal and mentally tell myself that what I had written on the paper was what I wanted my psychic mind to direct me to achieve. Then I would fold the paper, place it in the bowl and close the drawer.

As I drifted off to sleep, I mentally reviewed the goal to impress it on my mind. The very first goal I had put into the bowl was "I want to develop my innate psychic abilities."

Within a few weeks I had filled the bowl with a lot of goals, many of which were not especially important. Because of the volume of goals I had forgotten most of them and had lost my focus. It seemed obvious I needed a better method; my psychic mind was beginning to develop more and direct me toward where I needed to be.

Following the direction in which my psychic mind was leading me, I took all the goal notes out of the bowl and wrote just one goal which I placed in the bowl. The goal was "I want to find an effective method for me to set significant goals to program my higher mind that allows me to remain focused to ensure success."

Just two days later the concept flashed into my mind like a lightning bolt as I was about to drift off to sleep. I immediately put the concept into practice and have used it successfully ever since. I still call it my "Psychic Goal Bowl" even though it has nothing to do with goals written on notes in a cereal bowl anymore. Here is the method, which I offer for your consideration as a psychic goal-programming mechanism for your higher mind.

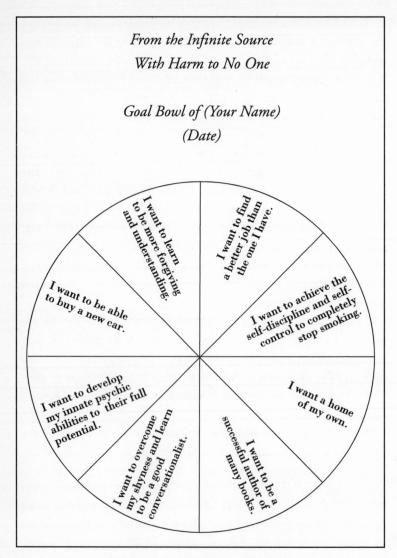

Figure 9-1. Sample Psychic Goal Bowl

First I took a sheet of typing paper and drew the largest circle I could. I divided the circle into eight pie-shaped sections, as shown in Figure 9-1.

I've included eight sample goals in Figure 9-1, one goal per pie-shaped section; these are not necessarily my goals, just examples to illustrate the psychic goal bowl concept. Shortly I'll tell you how to make a bowl with your own goals and program your psychic mind using the goal bowl. For the moment, just consider Figure 9-1 as a mechanism through which you can more effectively communicate with your higher mind.

Take notice of several salient features of the goal bowl. At the top, enter your name and the date you created the bowl. Notice two statements that you should put on your bowl: "With harm to no one" and "From the infinite source." These are extremely important.

The "with harm to no one" statement means that you do not want to achieve any goal if in doing so it would cause harm to you or to anyone else. To achieve a goal that causes harm would cause you to incur negative karma which you don't want to have to deal with. Let me tell you a story to illustrate this point.

Case #14

A Goal Gone Wrong

Some years ago a young man incurred a gambling debt of ten thousand dollars with some criminal characters. He couldn't pay the debt, so the criminals gave him a deadline by which he had to pay the money or they would kill him.

In desperation, the young man prayed day and night. He meditated. He pleaded with his higher mind. His prayers and pleading consisted of the words "I need ten thousand dollars now, before the deadline. Please enable me to get it." That was all. He repeated it aloud and mentally hundreds of times, programming his mind for his goal of obtaining ten thousand dollars quickly.

Several days later he achieved his goal. He was in an automobile accident and lost one arm and one leg. His insurance policy paid him five thousand dollars for each lost limb. He had his ten thousand dollars, but at a great personal price.

He had not put "with harm to no one" in his goal programming. The moral: Be careful what you ask for because you might get it. Be smart. Put the "with harm to no one" statement in all of your goals.

The "from the infinite source" statement recognizes that there is a power and intelligence greater than you as an individual and that you humble yourself before that power and intelligence when you ask help in achieving a goal.

Your goal bowl can contain pictures as well as words. In Figure 9-1, for example, you could include a photograph of the kind of house or car you need. The goal bowl can contain all pictures, or all words, or a combination of hand-drawn sketches, pictures and words. Communicate your goals to your higher mind in whatever way you find to be most effective. Quite often, a picture in combination with words helps you focus more powerfully on the goal. I recommend using pictures as much as possible.

You don't have to have eight segments in your goal bowl as shown in Figure 9-1. You can have only a circle encompassing just one goal, or divided in half for two goals. You can put in as many goal segments as you want, but you don't have to fill them all at the time you create your bowl; you can add more goals later.

First, give some serious thought to a goal, or several goals, that you really want to achieve. They can be long term goals or short term goals. The important thing is that in your heart you really want them and believe them to be beneficial to you, with harm to no one. Try not to be trivial or frivolous in your thinking.

Exercise #18
Creating Your Goal Bowl

- Once you have decided on your goals, draw a diagram similar to Figure 9-1. If you can find a picture (or draw a picture) of your goal, put it into one of the goal segments along with some words to define exactly what you want. Be as specific as possible.
- After you complete a goal section, look it over. Re-read it. Fix it in your mind.
- Close your eyes, go to your basic psychic level and visualize your goal.
- Say your goal out loud. For example: "I want to become the manager of my department at work" or "I want a new Jeep Cherokee™ automobile."
- Open your eyes and fill in your next goal segment using the same procedure just described above.
- Keep repeating the above steps for each goal segment in turn until you have filled in as many as you want.
- Once you have filled in as much of your goal bowl as you wish, re-read the entire bowl out loud, starting with the

title, date, harm to no one, infinite source, and continuing through each goal in turn. Pause to reflect briefly on each goal before proceeding to the next.

- After reviewing the entire goal bowl, close your eyes, go to your basic psychic level and say out loud, "The goals in my goal bowl are what I want, and I direct my higher mind to make these goals become reality."
- Put the goal bowl in a safe place, such as a personal drawer.
- For the first thirty days after you create your goal bowl, review it at least once each day as described above, except that you can go to your basic psychic level with your eyes open if you wish (as you learned to do in Exercise #10). Note: You can review your goal bowl as often as you wish, but do it at least once each day for the first thirty days.
- After the first thirty days, review your goal bowl as described at least once a month for the next twelve months.
- After the first year, review your goal bowl at least twice a year. The more often you review your goal bowl, the more powerfully you reinforce the programming of your higher mind.

You will find that your psychic mind will start guiding you in certain directions that will offer opportunities to achieve your goals. Sometimes your psychic mind will be so subtle that you will only recognize its work after you have achieved a goal. At other times your psychic mind's directions will be as obvious as a roll of thunder. Don't be concerned about how your psychic mind directs you. Just be content to know that it works the way it should.

When you find that you have achieved a goal, write "thank you" and any comments you wish in that segment of your psychic goal bowl. I recommend you write the date of your entry for future reference.

In some cases, you may change your mind about a goal. That is okay. If you want to cancel a goal, write "CANCEL" across that section of your goal bowl, and impress it on your mind as previously described. You may also want to date the entry and write why you are cancelling the goal.

One caution — if you find yourself frequently cancelling goals, it is a sign you may not be giving your goals serious thought before entering them into your goal bowl. Also, if you are frequently cancelling goals it signals your psychic mind not to take you seriously because you keep changing your mind. If that happens your psychic mind might shut down and not respond to any of your requests. This is serious business, so please approach it that way. Occasional cancellations or changes to your goal bowl will not cause a problem.

You may want to modify a goal. For example, you might want to change "graduate from college" to "graduate from drafting technical school." Just write in the change and impress it in your mind as previously described.

You can add additional goals whenever you wish. Use an additional goal bowl diagram if you need the extra space. I record no more than eight significant goals at one time, making a new one only when one of my old ones has been achieved, but that is my personal choice. You do what feels right for you. It is your psychic goal bowl, so make the rules that seem best for you.

Case #15

One of My Goals

In a goal bowl I made in the early 1970s, I drew a sketch of several books. The books had my name on them, but no titles. I wrote "I want to be a successful published professional author of books." At the time I had never written a book and had no ideas for a book.

Within a couple of months events occurred unexpectedly that changed the course of my life. The whole sequence of events spanned several years and led me to write a book entitled *Daydream Your Way To Success* (later retitled *Hypnosis*). More events took place. Today I have six successful books (counting this one) and several booklets on the market, and I am still writing. All I did was follow the exact psychic goal bowl procedure described in this chapter.

Using a goal bowl is not hocus-pocus. To become a writer I had to learn how to write. I had to study. I had to prepare myself. That was all part of the direction my psychic mind commanded me to follow. Rarely does one get something for nothing.

If you want to win at the slot machines, you first have to invest some quarters. So don't expect your goal bowl to hand your goal to you with no effort on your part. What you can expect is that your goal bowl (higher, psychic mind) will direct you to take actions that will result in your achieving your goal. Don't expect freebees; if you do get a freebee, give thanks and feel privileged, because freebees are rare.

Case #16

Thomas Edison's Psychic Goal

Thomas Edison had a goal: to create an electric light bulb. Every moment of every day he impressed that goal on his mind. His psychic mind directed him to perform over nine thousand experiments before he found the solution that would work: a tungsten filament in a vacuum, enclosed in glass. Edison lit up the world.

You probably won't have to labor through nine thousand tries before achieving your goals, but you will have to impress your goal bowl on your mind and you will have to cooperate with the direction your psychic mind gives you.

Here is something I do that you may want to try. I spend a dime or two at a local print shop to make a photocopy reduction of my goal bowl. I reduce it to about twenty-five percent of its original size. It is still perfectly legible, but small enough to be folded and easily carried in a wallet or purse. This way I always have it with me to review any time.

For example, when sitting in a waiting room (doctor, dentist, other appointment) I can pull out the small version of my goal bowl and review it, reinforcing my psychic programming. I travel a lot and review my small goal bowl on the airplane and in hotel and motel rooms. If you want to succeed and achieve, take every opportunity to program your psychic mind with your goal bowl objectives.

The psychic goal bowl concept works, and it keeps you out of the garbage pile.

■ ■

Chapter 10

CLAIRVOYANCE

Nearly all psychic work involves clairvoyance.

Clairvoyance — The power to perceive things outside of the natural range of human senses. Acute intuitive insight or perceptiveness.

Prophesy — Foreseeing the future. To predict. This is really a subset of clairvoyance and is discussed in this chapter as part of clairvoyance.

Clairvoyance in its most primitive form is just a powerful "feeling" that something is, or is not, going to happen. It is probably an innate clairvoyant ability that allowed primitive humans to survive and prosper. As humans progressed and learned to speak and write and draw, they became less dependent on their innate clairvoyant ability and more on their new-found communications skills.

Today modern communications are so sophisticated, and our social laws and practices so stylized, that few people pay any attention at all to innate clairvoyant ability. We think that only a select few have the special ability to foresee events. The truth is that we all have some clairvoyant ability, but it has been driven deep inside by lack of use, fear of ridicule, and ignorance.

We all have hunches from time to time, and hunches are the tip of the clairvoyant iceberg; hunches are a throwback to the dawn of humanity. Yet most people ignore their hunches. Every time you ignore a hunch you are telling your higher mind, "I don't want to be clairvoyant." Eventually you drive your natural clairvoyance so deep that it may be very difficult to retrieve.

I personally believe that clairvoyance is the most important of the psychic abilities and that it is also the one that is naturally most common in people.

Here is a case of clairvoyance and prophesy.

Case #17
The Locomotive

Not all psychic experiences are profound. Many are just strong feelings or hunches about something.

In 1964, my wife and I and our three young children lived in a small town in upstate New York. The activities of the town centered around the local Veterans of Foreign Wars (VFW) organization which was very active. The VFW had purchased an old steam locomotive and refurbished it to use in parades. They put in a gasoline engine, outfitted it with heavy duty truck tires, and remodeled the coal tender with seats for passengers. The official driver (I'll call him Nelson) was a friend of ours.

Nelson pulled up in front of our house in the locomotive one day. On board were his wife and another couple we knew casually. He wanted us to come aboard and go for a joy ride. My wife and children were ecstatic as I helped them board.

Just as I started to step up into the tender, a powerful feeling of apprehension gripped me. I knew there was going to be an accident.

I quickly stepped back to the ground. My wife and children refused to get off. Everyone jeered that I was a "party pooper." They drove off.

By the time I got my car out of the garage, the locomotive had disappeared over a hill. I followed.

At the first curve after topping the hill, I caught up with them. The locomotive was in a ditch after first sheering off a telephone pole. The woman who was sitting next to my wife was bleeding profusely from the head. Apparently a piece of the damaged telephone pole had hit her. Thankfully, no one else was hurt.

I took the woman for medical attention and transported everyone else to her house for an impromptu party. The woman's cut was not serious, and she also joined the party. All in all, it wasn't a serious matter.

Then why did I get the psychic warning? Probably to protect me. It is likely that if I had boarded the locomotive I would have been sitting in the woman's place, next to my wife. Hence, I would likely have been injured.

When I reflect over my life, I can count dozens of times when I was protected either by a psychic experience or by a freak set of circumstances. I won't belabor all of them with you. This one incident describes quite well a subtle kind of psychic experience for benefit. Higher mind seems to do an excellent job of taking care of me. It will for you, too, if you allow it.

Many of the other examples in the book have elements of clairvoyance in them. For example, if you want to do psychic healing you have a better chance if you are clairvoyant. Mental telepathy goes hand in hand with clairvoyance; sometimes the line between clairvoyance and telepathy becomes fuzzy.

There is one thing you must start doing one hundred percent of the time if you want to be an excellent clairvoyant. Pay attention to your hunches and feelings. Each time you do you are telling your mind, "I want to be clairvoyant."

One enjoyable way to develop your clairvoyant ability is to learn to read tea leaves. It is simple and lots of fun.* That is how I got started. My mother, a gifted psychic, was the town tea leaf reader when I was a child. She taught me how to read tea leaves when I was about eleven years old. Reading tea leaves will help bring out and sharpen whatever natural clairvoyant ability you have.

Once you have sharpened your clairvoyant ability using the techniques described in this book you will find that all you need to do is relax and focus your awareness on your desire to know information and it will be given to you. Knowledge will flow freely into your mind. You will have bunches of hunches.

There can be a down side to clairvoyance, and I want to make you aware of it so you will be able to handle it. The drawback is that you will start to know more than you want to know.

In the early and mid-1970s that happened to me. I had been working as a professional psychic and I got so keen that I began knowing things about people, things I had no right to know and didn't want to know. That is a heavy burden to bear.

I sat down in private and used self-hypnosis techniques to reprogram my mind so that my clairvoyance would work only if there was a need for me to know. Thus, if someone asked me

---

* My book, *Tea Leaf Reading* (Llewellyn Publications) teaches you how with step-by-step instructions.

what happened to their missing dog, I would perceive only information needed to answer the question — I would not automatically also know all about the person's sex life, or that she was stealing from her employer.

Perhaps you may not feel burdened by knowing all those things, but I did. Since I reprogrammed my mind I feel much better about using clairvoyance.

I get spontaneous clairvoyant impressions all the time that are beneficial for me to know. The following are some recent examples.

1. A car mechanic tried to rip me off by telling me I needed a new alternator on my car. He said he could replace it for $160. My mind shouted to me, "No, he is lying!" I simply said, "I want to think about it." Then I went to another auto service center and was told my alternator was fine, but that someone had disconnected my voltage regulator, which would give the appearance of a defective alternator. I had listened to my mind and saved $160.

2. On a tour of a company with which I have a financial relationship, I met the entire staff. Two of the people, the sales manager and one other key person, gave me powerful negative feelings the moment I shook hands with them. I knew instantly that they were incompetent and harmful to the company. I had no hard proof — only a powerful clairvoyant awareness. I knew was right, but of course I had to keep my mouth shut. All I could do was conduct my relationships with them in a careful manner. Before many months had passed the company became aware of the problems with the two people and separated them from the company. Unfortunately, they had caused serious financial harm before being found out.

3. One day my mind directed me to go to a specific automobile dealer on a certain day in order to purchase a new vehicle at a "steal" price. I did, and saved $7000. Two weeks later, the dealer unexpectedly closed his doors forever.

Being at the right place at the right time is something that happens to me so frequently that I accept it as a normal event. My mind speaks of things I have no normal way of knowing about, and I listen. That is clairvoyance.

Here are four exercises to sharpen and test your clairvoyance and prophesy skills. They test your skills at the time you perform the exercises, so expect your results to vary from time to time. They also sharpen your psychic abilities each time you perform the exercises.

Exercise #19

Dictionary Divination

- Get a dictionary and hold it in your lap or place it on a table in front of you, as you choose.
- Close your eyes and go to your basic psychic level.
- With your eyes still closed, ask any question, out loud, to which you wish to find the answer.
- Then, keeping your eyes closed, riffle through the dictionary pages until you feel you have reached the place that might have the answer you seek. You may need to riffle front to back and back to front a number of times before you feel you have reached the place where the answer to your question can be found.

At the moment you feel you have reached the right place, stop riffling the pages and place the tip of your finger somewhere on either of the two open pages. Choose whatever feels to you to be the appropriate spot.

- Keeping your finger on that spot, open your eyes and read the definitions of the word to which your finger is pointing. Somewhere within the context of the definition will be the answer, or a clue to the answer, of your question.

Here is an example of what could happen. Suppose you asked, "What would be my future as a professional writer?"

You riffle the pages and point. When you open your eyes your finger is on the definition of the word "pittance."

One of the definitions of pittance in the dictionary is "scanty income or remuneration." So it is clear that your answer is that you would make very little money from writing if you chose to be a writer.

Try dictionary divination a few times. It is good psychic practice and you can gain valuable information.

I recommend that you keep a log book of your questions and the dictionary's answers for future reference as your life evolves. One reason for this is that you may not understand the dictionary's answer at the time, but as later events occur in your life you will be able to see how accurate the dictionary was. Such a log book is a good psychic tool.

Exercise #20

Pendulum Divination

Initial Preparation:

- Make yourself a pendulum. Use a thread or light string about ten inches long and tie a light weight at one end of the string; a small metal nut or bolt will do fine. You need a weight so the pendulum can swing, but you don't want it so heavy that it takes a forty-mile-per-hour wind to cause the pendulum to move.
- Next draw a diagram (similar to the one in Figure 10-1) on a sheet of writing paper.
- Lay the paper on a table and hold your pendulum by the end of the thread so the weight is suspended over (but not touching) the intersection of the two lines.
- Go to your basic psychic level with your eyes open.
- Deliberately cause the pendulum to swing in the "yes" direction.

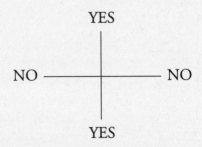

Figure 10-1. Pendulum Diagram

- Say out loud, "This is the direction in which I want the pendulum to swing when the correct answer to any question I ask is 'yes'."
- Then deliberately cause the pendulum to swing in the "no" direction.
- Say out loud, "This is the direction in which I want the pendulum to swing when the correct answer to any question I ask is 'no'."

Divination Exercise:

- Cause the pendulum to be still (not swaying). Hold the end of the thread without moving your hand.
- Ask out loud any question you wish that can be answered by either "yes" or "no." Continue holding the thread very still. Soon the pendulum will begin to swing all by itself, without your moving your hand.
- If the pendulum swings in the direction of the "yes" line, "yes" is the answer to your question. If it swings in the direction of the "no" line, "no" is the answer to your question.
- If the pendulum swings in a circle, your question either cannot be answered at this time because of reasons that cosmic consciousness is deliberately withholding from you, or you have asked too complex a question; the answer cannot be given as a simple yes or no.

For example, suppose you asked, "Would it be a beneficial career move for me to accept the job offer from Apex Corp?" You would get a clear-cut yes or no answer.

However, suppose you asked, "Should I take the offer from Apex on a temporary basis while looking for something better, or should I stick with my current job a while longer?" The pendulum would go in a circle because it is unable to answer this question with a simple yes or no.

Pendulum divination is fun, and you will be surprised at what you learn. Your psychic mind is in action in this divination exercise.

You might want to keep a log book of questions asked, the dates, and the pendulum's answers, then observe what actually evolves in your life.

Exercise #21

Card/Colors Divination

Initial Preparation:

- Obtain a deck of regular playing cards. Each deck has twenty-six red cards and twenty-six black cards.
- Shuffle the deck of cards and place the deck face down on the table.

Card/Colors Exercise:

- Go to your basic psychic level with your eyes open.
- Mark on a paper what you think the color of the top card is (red or black). Then turn the card over and set it aside to see if you are correct. Mark on a paper each time you are correct.

Go through the entire deck of fifty-two cards in this manner, and then total up your score to see how many you had correct.

If you got more than twenty-six correct, you were displaying psychic ability; the higher the score, the more psychic sensitivity is indicated.

I recommend that you do this exercise four times during one sitting to get a more accurate picture of how much psychic ability you are displaying.

Typically, when I do this the first time I might get twenty-eight cards correct, the second time perhaps thirty-five, the third time thirty-two, and the fourth time only eighteen because my mind is getting bored.

Exercise #22

Card/Symbols Divination

Initial Preparation:

- Using a standard deck of fifty-two playing cards you are now going to use your psychic sense to predict the symbols on the cards. Each deck of cards has four symbols (thirteen cards of each symbol): Heart, Spade, Diamond, and Club.
- Shuffle the deck and place it face down on the table in front of you.

Card/Symbols Exercise:

- Go to your basic psychic level with your eyes open.
- On a paper write down what you think the top card symbol is.
- Then turn the card over and set it aside, writing down whether or not you were correct.

Go through the entire deck one card at a time, predicting what the symbol on the top card is and then making note of whether or not you were correct.

At the end, total your correct answers. If you got more than thirteen correct answers you were displaying accurate psychic sensing.

I recommend that you do this game at least four times at a sitting in order to get a more accurate picture of how well your psychic sense is functioning.

■ ■

Chapter 11

TELEPATHY

Telepathy — Communication through means other than the senses, as by the exercise of mystical powers.

Mind Reading — To detect what is in someone's mind by using mystical powers. Mind reading is a subset of telepathy and will be discussed here as a part of telepathy.

Telepathy is the act of mentally receiving information from or sending information to someone's mind.

Telepathy may be spontaneous or it may be deliberate. Perhaps your spouse falls down the stairs at home and is injured and unable to move. He or she calls, "Help!" either mentally or out loud. At work you hear that plea in your mind; you know something is wrong, so you rush home and are able to help your mate. That is an example of spontaneous telepathy. Your minds made a connection by inexplicable means. These things happen every day, all over the world.

Deliberate telepathy occurs when you and another person intentionally transmit mental messages to each other.

You can train your mind by deliberately practicing with other people, using a deck of cards.

Exercise #23

Telepathy Training

- To train for telepathy, one person (the Sender) looks at a card face and concentrates on mentally sending that image to another person (the Receiver).
- The Receiver writes down the impression he or she receives.
- At the end of one run through the deck, the Receiver compares notes with the Sender to determine how accurately the images were conveyed from one to the other.
- Then the two people reverse roles so that each one has a chance to send and to receive.

After three or so runs through the deck mental boredom usually sets in and it is wise to take a break.

Some people are better senders than receivers and *vice versa.* Some are equally adept at both sending and receiving.

You also can practice long distance. For example, you and a friend can agree to sit down at a specific time in your respective homes, no matter how far apart you are. One will send a picture for five minutes. Then the other will send a picture for five minutes. Then, compare notes to see how well you did. If you live in different time zones, be sure to take that into account when you arrange your practice time.

Suppose your friend concentrates on a picture of a chestnut horse and you get the impression of a large brown animal, but nothing more specific. Count that as a hit; you were picking up valid information even though you did not pick up everything. With diligent practice, you will improve your ability to sense more detail.

You can devise an infinite number of mental exercises to develop your telepathic ability. Use your imagination.

Telepathy, like clairvoyance, plays a big role in most psychic work, and many of the case studies in this book contain elements of telepathy.

■ ■

Chapter 12

Psychometry

Psychometry is basically clairvoyance implemented by, or triggered by, the sense of touch. In other words, it is the ability to sense information from objects by physically touching them.

To learn this skill, select one or more objects. As you hold or touch each one, alter your consciousness to your basic psychic level and try to sense information from them.

Psychometry is a great skill to have and it is well worth the time to develop it.

Here is how to tune up your psychometry senses, using a standard deck of cards.

Exercise #24

Psychometry Tune-Up

Tune-Up:
- Place the deck in front of you and pick up the top card.
- Go to your basic psychic level with your eyes open.
- Look at the card to see what color it is. Feel the card. Repeat the color, out loud and mentally.
- Close your eyes and visualize the color while rubbing the colored side of the card with your fingers.
- Say to yourself (out loud or mentally as you wish), "This is how the color (name the color) feels, and I will recognize

the color (name of color) whenever I feel it with my hands or fingers in the future."

- Go through the entire deck in this manner.
- In the case of a standard card deck you are now attuned to the colors red and black.
- If you have a deck of cards with dots or symbols on them in a variety of colors, use the same tune-up procedure. The advantage of such a deck is that you get to tune up on more than just two colors.
- If you really want a challenging tune-up using a standard deck of playing cards, you would say something like, "This is how the black Queen of Spades feels, and I will recognize the black color, and the symbol of spades, and the image of a queen, whenever I encounter any of them with my hands or fingers in the future." Continue through the entire deck in this manner.

Testing:

- When you are ready to test yourself, shuffle the deck and place it face down.
- Go to your basic psychic level with your eyes open.
- Pick up one card at a time. Hold and feel it without looking at what is imprinted on it.
- Write down your impression.
- Check to see if you were correct.

Keep track of your correct hits; your score at the end will indicate how well you are doing.

These tune-up exercises are useful, but don't get discouraged if you get a low score. A low score does not mean that you will never be good at psychometry. I do much better in actual performance on a real case than I do in practice tune-up sessions. I suspect that is because my mind considers a real case to be more important than a practice exercise and thus functions accurately a higher percentage of the time when it really matters.

After you have completed the tune-up exercise you should start practicing with real objects. You might want to start with an object worn or handled a great deal by someone you already know. Examples might include your mother's wristwatch or your father's pocketknife.

You will be sensing things you already know about the owner. Because you already know that your mother is kind and loving and a good cook, you think about those things as you hold her watch. What you are doing is sensitizing your psychic awareness to associate what you know to be true with the subtle energies you sense through your fingers and hands.

Continue to practice with other objects in the same manner. Always keep your awareness open for information you didn't know. Gradually, wean yourself away from objects possessed by people you know to those of which you have no knowledge.

If you find a coin or object on the street, try to read knowledge from it by holding it. See what you can read (feel) from the walls and furnishings in buildings.

If you have an opportunity to visit a genuine haunted house, do so. The energies you can pick up by touching walls and other objects can be awe-inspiring.

The key to performing successful psychometry is to just keep doing it. Practice, along with innate ability, is the key to success.

The following case history started with the use of psychometry, but it also illustrates mental projection, telepathy, communication with an entity, and probably a couple of other things. I use it here because it does illustrate psychometry quite well.

Case #18 _____

Murder Investigation

I am deliberately vague about names, dates, gender (I refer to the victim without sexual identification), and some other physical specifics, to insure that no one involved can be identified. My intention is to protect them from concern and embarrassment. I have not altered any facts.

This case shows how you can muster a variety of psychic abilities to solve a practical problem.

I was giving a series of lectures on psychic matters. After one lecture, a woman in the audience approached me. She asked if I could really get information by touching objects. I said I had had some success with psychometry but hadn't done a lot of it. She thanked me and left.

She returned to the following night's lecture. Afterward, she again approached me.

"My husband is the homicide detective in charge of the investigation of a brutal murder," she said. "The police are holding the person they are certain is the murderer, on a charge of weapons possessions, but without physical evidence to substantiate a murder charge, they will have to release the person in another forty-eight hours. My husband knows that the person will disappear immediately if released. If that happens, justice may never be served."

She paused while she searched through her purse. Extracting a map, she unfolded it.

"I told my husband about you," she continued. "He can use all the help he can get."

"How can I help?"

"My husband marked on the map where the body was found. Can you use psychometry to detect anything about the murder?"

"I don't know, but I will give it my best shot. No promises, though."

Standing there, I placed my right index finger on the mark on the map. I closed my eyes and went to my basic psychic level. Slowly, I moved my finger around. For a minute or so, nothing happened.

Then a vehicle appeared on my mental movie screen, and I described it to her: color, body style, even some paint scratches on one side.

"What about the bullet?" she asked. "The bullet went through the body and has not been found. The bullet is the physical evidence we need. Where is it?"

"About a hundred yards north-northeast from the body in a clump of trees," I responded immediately because I saw it on my screen.

After that, I received nothing. She thanked me and left.

At eight o'clock the next morning her husband phoned me. He asked if I would meet him at the murder scene and gave me directions.

"Be sure to wear boots," he advised. "It is very muddy out there."

The murder scene was in a rural area that I had never been to before. The detective was waiting for me with a metal detector in hand.

The area was cordoned off with crime scene warnings. Little red flags were stuck in the ground where the body, and pieces of brain and bone, had been found. It was the pattern of these pieces of brain and bone that led investigators to believe the bullet had traveled in a northwest direction. Using metal detectors, they had searched to the northwest for the bullet, in vain.

The detective was warm and friendly. He looked more like a college football player than a policeman.

"Your description of the suspect's vehicle was a hundred percent accurate," he told me. "But you said the bullet traveled north-northeast. Our lab people disagree. And as you can see, there is no clump of trees in that direction."

He was right. I looked out over the barren field. There wasn't a tree in sight. Yet I had seen it clearly. And now, standing where the body had lain, I felt even more strongly about it. I was getting very strong feelings and images from my physical contact with the ground where the victim had died.

I began walking in the direction that I felt was correct, staying at my basic psychic level. The detective slogged along with me through the mud.

About a hundred or so yards out, we came to a sharp dip in the terrain. At the bottom of the dip was a clump of felled trees and bushes forming a pile about three feet high and twenty feet in diameter. Viewed from the place where the body had lain, the trees were completely hidden.

"Well, I'll ..." the detective muttered.

He immediately went to work with his metal detector. I watched silently. There was no way he could penetrate the mass of brush and wood, and there was neither time nor manpower to clear it away. Only twenty-four hours were left now before the suspect would have to be released.

The detective was frustrated. "Damn! I know the bullet is in there, and I can't get to it. I know you are right. Damn!"

"The bullet will never be found," I said. "It is too deep in the mud to be detected. Let me try a different approach."

We returned to the murder site. Still at my basic psychic level I asked the deceased victim to enter my mental awareness and to communicate with me.

The victim was confused about what had happened, but after a brief interaction I was assured that the guilty person was the one being held in jail.

"I can't go into court with that."

"I know," I said, "but now at least we know for sure that you are holding the right person."

"So what? We have to release the suspect in about twenty-four hours. We don't have the physical evidence to hold the suspect longer than that."

"Give me a moment," I said.

Still at my psychic level, I called the suspect into my mental awareness, where I did a psychic reading. Finished, I exited my psychic level.

"I think you have a chance that the suspect will solve the case for you," I said. "I did a reading on the suspect and found out several very interesting things."

"Like what?"

"First, the suspect is of below-average intelligence. Second, the suspect is gloating inwardly about committing the perfect crime and making the police look like fools. Third, the suspect has an insatiable ego. The suspect loves recognition and praise, and wants someone to recognize his cleverness."

"So?"

"I strongly sense that he will confess to someone he considers safe, someone who will praise him."

"How? When? And suppose he doesn't confess?"

"If he is going to confess, I think it will be very soon. If not, I guess he will go free, even though you know he is guilty."

The news on the radio the next day told the rest of the story. Around nine the previous night, the suspect had bragged about the murder in full detail to the prisoner in the adjacent cell. That morning the prisoner, who was being held on several theft charges, called the guard and offered to exchange testimony against the murder suspect in exchange for a reduction of the theft charges. The District Attorney agreed, and this was sufficient to bind the murder suspect over for trial. Result: Conviction and a prison sentence.

This the only criminal investigation in which I have helped simply because it is the only time I have been asked to help.

I have tried to solve crimes without being asked, but have not been successful. I have found that when I am asked to do something, my psychic powers seem to intensify and become keen and I am able to perform quite well. When I do not have a request, I do not always get good results. That is just me. That is not necessarily you. Find out for yourself what you can do.

■ ■

Chapter 13

ASTRAL TRAVEL

Some people are able to leave their bodies, travel to distant places, and bring back information gained from their excursions. They can do this while awake and conscious; they do it at will. Other people do it spontaneously; that is, they have not learned to control it. It just happens, without warning.

Most people are like me. We go on occasional out-of-body excursions while asleep, and awake later with a recollection of the experience. I have not yet learned how to travel out-of-body while awake, so I am not able to teach you how. What I do is mentally project myself to where I want to be, which is the technique I teach in this book.

I have had one unusual out-of-body encounter, which I will share with you.

Case #19

Out-of-Body Encounter

One of my early psychic teachers was a very pretty young woman named Marcia. She was a natural psychic and had been doing out-of-body (astral) travel at will for as long as she could remember. She was in her teens before she realized that she was unusual; that not everyone was like her.

Marcia was conducting a series of lectures, which I attended.

She had taught us how to reach theta, and we were all in that state, eyes closed, while she talked to us from the front of the room.

I heard her voice move to the side of the room and then down to where I was seated. Then, in an instant, her voice was inside my head, and my entire body felt bloated. After about fifteen seconds, her voice moved to the front of the room, and I no longer felt bloated.

She had us open our eyes.

"Did anyone have any unusual experiences in theta?" she asked.

No hands went up. I knew I should have raised my hand, but I thought I was being foolish.

"Yes. One person did have an unusual experience," Marcia continued. "Will you tell us about it, Bill?"

"So it wasn't my imagination," I said, and related my experience.

Marcia smiled. She explained that she had gone out of body, walked over to me (while her physical body remained at the front of the room), and sat down inside my body for a short while.

I have half-heartedly tried astral travel techniques as described in several books, with no success. Probably my lack of natural ability in this one psychic area, plus my lack of persistence in practicing, account for my lack of success. Also, my Spirit Guide advised me that there was no need for me to perform out-of-body travel, and I always heed advice from my Spirit Guide.

Since she was about two years old, Marcia had always been able to astral travel, at will. It was a natural ability. She didn't know how to teach it to me because she performed astral travel simply by desiring it. For her, astral travel required no more effort than a passing thought.

If having out-of-body travel with conscious awareness is something that interests you, search the library or book stores for books that can give you greater knowledge of the subject.

Ask your Spirit Guide if this is a beneficial course for you to follow. If your Spirit Guide says "Yes," ask your Spirit Guide to lead you to the method for making astral travel happen. Follow wherever your Spirit Guide directs you. You may get an immediate response. You may be led to meet someone who can teach you, or you may be led to a book that can teach you. Be patient, have faith, and don't give up.

■ ■

Chapter 14

THE BEACH OF TIME

In your psychic work you will not be constrained by time boundaries. While you physically live in the present time and a specific location, in the psychic world it is a different story.

Your psychic mind can travel to any point in the universe in the present, past, and future.

To assist you in your psychic travel, you will be introduced to the Beach of Time on the shores of the Sea of Cosmic Consciousness. While on the Beach of Time, you will be able to function psychically at any point in time and space. The Beach of Time exists at a psychic level of your mind different from your basic psychic level.

Exercise #25

Going to the Beach of Time

- Sit in a comfortable, quiet place. Take the phone off the hook.
- Close your eyes and go to your basic psychic level.
- Say to yourself, "I will now go to the Beach of Time by counting down from five to one." Mentally count down: 5-4-3-2-1. At the count of one, visualize a white sand beach on the edge of a deep blue sea. The sea is calm and peaceful. The white beach stretches to your left and to your right.

- You are standing in the present time on the Beach of Time on the shores of the infinitely huge Sea of Cosmic Consciousness.
- Spend a few moments enjoying the beauty and warmth of this magnificent place. Feel the peacefulness.
- Turn and look to the right. This is the direction of time past. A short distance from you, time past is concealed by a fog bank.
- Now turn and look to the left. This is the direction of time future. A short distance from you, time future is concealed by a fog bank.
- Mentally say to yourself, "I can return here to the Beach of Time any time I wish simply by closing my eyes, going to my basic psychic level, and then counting from five down to one."
- Now, as you count from one up to five, the Beach of Time disappears from your mental vision.
- Open your eyes.

You have now discovered a powerful and valuable level of your psychic mind that you can use whenever you wish.

Exercise #26

Going Psychically into the Past

- Relax in a comfortable place.
- Close your eyes.
- Go to your basic psychic level.
- Go to the Beach of Time using the 5-4-3-2-1 countdown.
- Turn to your right and walk into the fog bank.

- Once in the fog bank, direct your mind to go wherever you wish in the past by saying something like, "I want to return to my third birthday."
- The fog bank will evaporate and you will find yourself in the appropriate time in the past.
- To leave the past and return to the Beach of Time, say to yourself, "I now wish to return to the Beach of Time present," and allow the fog to envelop you.
- Walk to your left out of the fog and into the present time on the beach.
- Count up 1-2-3-4-5 and the Beach of Time disappears.
- Open your eyes.

Exercise #27

Going Psychically into the Future

- Relax in a comfortable place.
- Close your eyes.
- Go to your basic psychic level.
- Go to the Beach of Time, using the 5-4-3-2-1 countdown.
- Turn to your left and walk into the fog bank.
- Once in the fog bank, direct your mind to go wherever you wish in the future by saying something like "I want to go to the North Pole on January 1, 2020."
- The fog will evaporate and you will find yourself in the appropriate time in the future.
- To leave the future and return to the Beach of Time, say to yourself, "I now wish to return to the Beach of Time present," and allow the fog to envelop you.

- Walk to your right out of the fog and into the present time on the beach.
- Count up 1-2-3-4-5 and the Beach of Time disappears.
- Open your eyes.

To do psychic work in the present time, just go to the Beach of Time and perform whatever psychic work you wish.

When you are on the Beach of Time, it would be a good idea to ask your Guardian Angel to instantly bring you back to the present time with your eyes open in the event of an emergency requiring your immediate attention, such as a neighbor's house on fire.

As you can see, these psychic exercises are becoming more profound, interesting, and a bit more complex. You are progressing nicely.

Anything you can do at your basic psychic level you can also do on the Beach of Time. The Beach of Time provides a more powerful level from which to perform time travel, prayer, meditation, consulting with cosmic consciousness, or other psychic procedures that consume more time than you generally need when using your basic level.

I probably use my basic psychic level ninety percent of the time, reserving the Beach of Time for when I want to relax and interact for long periods with cosmic consciousness.

As you practice with the Beach of Time and with your basic psychic level, you will decide for yourself when you prefer to use the Beach of Time.

Meditation is a powerful tool for communicating with cosmic consciousness, and the Beach of Time is an especially powerful place to be to perform that meditation.

I do most of my meditation in the bathtub. The warm water relaxes me and adds physical reality to the Sea of Cosmic Consciousness, the place I mentally go to do my meditation.

To meditate, I go to the Beach of Time and wade out into the Sea of Cosmic Consciousness until the water is up to my chin. I feel the energy and joy of life flow into my body; the bathtub water adds realistic physical feeling to give more power to my meditation. You might also want to try this.

Meditation can serve either of two purposes:

1. It allows you to open your mind to receive energy, information, and guidance from cosmic consciousness.
2. It allows you to send psychic thoughts for a specific purpose.

I recommend that you start today, and continue every day, to use the Beach of Time to receive and send psychic thoughts. In so doing, you will open all the doors of your psychic mind, will enrich your life and the lives of others, and will develop into the very best person you are capable of becoming.

Here are a few more of the many things you may want to do on the Beach of Time.

- Pray. The power of your prayers is greatly intensified here.
- Contact deceased love ones.
- Project health and healing to others and to yourself.
- Practice psychometry by holding or feeling an object while allowing the object to give you information such as who owns the object, where the object came from, age of the object, and so forth.

- Solve problems. Ask your Spirit Guide and cosmic consciousness for help. This is probably the most practical and widely used purpose of psychic power.
- Send love and help to people.
- Ask for guidance in life.

Of course, you can also use your basic psychic level for many of the above functions, but the Beach of Time level is usually more powerful. Your basic psychic level is a bit faster and more convenient to use, especially if you are not in a position to close your eyes (while driving a car, for example). See what works best for you.

Summary

All you have to do to reach the Beach of Time is:

- Close your eyes.
- Go to your basic psychic level.
- Count from five down to one, and the beach and the sea are there.

To return from the Beach of Time:

- Count up from one to five; the beach and sea will disappear.
- Open your eyes.

You will now have the opportunity to perform four different psychic investigations on the Beach of Time to find out four important pieces of information that will help you.

You are completely on your own with these exercises. Unless you try things on your own, you will not progress as well as you are capable of progressing.

Do not combine these exercises into one; that might muddle up the information you receive. In addition, you need the experience of performing multiple psychic excursions to the Beach of Time.

Exercise #28

Finding Your Career Path

- Go to the Beach of Time.
- Walk out into the Sea of Cosmic Consciousness until the water is approximately up to your waist.
- Ask cosmic consciousness "What is the best career path for me to pursue at the present time?"
- Ask as many related questions as you wish.
- Stay for as long as you desire.
- Return from the Beach of Time when you are finished and open your eyes.
- Write down the awareness you received during this exercise.

Exercise #29

Finding the Best Use of Your Psychic Abilities

- Go to the Beach of Time.
- Walk out into the Sea of Cosmic Consciousness until the water is approximately up to your waist.
- Ask cosmic consciousness "How can I make the best use of my psychic abilities?"
- Ask as many related questions as you wish.
- Stay for as long as you desire.

- Return from the Beach of Time when you are finished and open your eyes.
- Write down the awareness you received during this exercise.

Exercise #30

Consulting with Your Spirit Guide & Guardian Angel

- Go to the Beach of Time.
- Sit down in the sand near the edge of the Sea of Cosmic Consciousness.
- Ask your Spirit Guide and Guardian Angel to meet you on the Beach of Time.
- Ask them to position themselves next to you, one on each side.
- Spend as much time as you wish communicating with your Spirit Guide and Guardian Angel.
- Ask them any questions you wish. Ask them for advice.
- Be sure to ask how you can quickly contact your Spirit Guide and Guardian Angel in the future
- When you are finished, say "Thank You" to your Spirit Guide and Guardian Angel.
- Return from the Beach of Time and open your eyes.
- Write down what happened.

Exercise #31

Asking for Help

- Select something with which you would like your Spirit Guide or Guardian Angel to help you. For example, you might ask, "Help me with my psychic development so that I may become the very best psychic I can be."
- Contact your Spirit Guide or Guardian Angel, using whatever method they suggested during your meeting in Exercise #30.
- Ask your question.
- Thank your Spirit Guide or Guardian Angel.
- Use your procedure to leave and open your eyes.
- Write down what occurred.

Much of your future psychic functioning may involve interaction with your Spirit Guide or Guardian Angel. This has been a very important psychic training exercise for you.

Do not hesitate to consult with your Spirit Guide or Guardian Angel often, even if just to say "Thanks" for their being with you.

■ ■

Chapter 15

COMMUNICATION WITH PEOPLE

Communicating with people is an extremely valuable application of your psychic abilities. It is most useful when there is some sort of barrier between you and the person with whom you wish to communicate. Using your psychic abilities, you can go to your basic psychic level with your eyes open and mentally talk to, and ask questions of, the person you have in mind. Since you will be communicating with that person at their subconscious level, you will receive truthful answers and will achieve remarkable results. Here are just three examples of such applications. In reality, there are probably a nearly infinite number of occasions to use this ability.

Case #20 _____

Ask a Salesperson for the Truth

I was dealing with a car salesman on the purchase of a new car, and I had a strong feeling he was lying to me about the actual cost of the car and about the finance charges. But every time I asked him, he gave me a line of double-talk and vague answers. I couldn't pin him down.

So I went to my basic psychic level with my eyes open and asked for the truth. I immediately got an awareness of exactly what to do.

The solution was very simple. I took a piece of paper and wrote down what I expected the proper purchase price, interest rate, and monthly payments should be. At the bottom of the paper I wrote, "The above statements are one hundred percent accurate and truthful and there are no additional costs or charges of any kind. The total cost of (description of car) is ($xx,xxx).

I then handed him the paper and asked him to sign and date it.

He refused.

So I turned and walked away while he followed me, trying to double-talk his way out of it.

Of course, I did not buy from him that day, nor have I ever gone back to that dealership.

You can avoid a lot of trouble if you use your psychic ability to ask for the truth.

Case #21
Difficult People

Have a frank talk with someone with whom you are having difficulty communicating. Some examples might be a boss who you feel has been unreasonable or unfair; a spouse, friend, or lover with whom you have had an argument; any person who is just plain "bull-headed" about some issue.

Usually these are situations where emotions get in the way of good communication.

The solution is to go to your basic psychic level or to the Beach of Time and invite the person into your mental vision. Then have a long, unemotional, frank discussion about everything. Give them a no-nonsense lecture if that seems appropriate.

This will bring amazing results quite quickly. You will enjoy watching the changes in other people when you use these methods.

Another great ploy to soften someone else's wrath or anger is to go to your basic psychic level (eyes open) and mentally say "I love you!" over and over while they are raising heck with you. You will see them grow uneasy, start to stammer, cool down, and maybe even apologize.

Case #22 ─────────────────────────────

Meeting the Right Person for You

Love, or the promise of it, is what makes the world go 'round. At some time in your life you might encounter some person you would like to get to know but, as happens to many people, for some reason or the other you can't seem to strike up an acquaintance. Perhaps you are too shy. Perhaps the other person is was too busy. Or maybe you just don't know how to arrange the meeting.

Whatever the obstacle, using your psychic ability allows you to get to know that "special" person.

There are several ways to arrange a meeting. You can go to your basic psychic level or to the Beach of Time, bring the person into your psychic awareness (vision) and talk to him or her.

Tell the person you would like a chance to meet. Ask the person to start paying attention to you, and so forth.

Also, every time you see the person, even at a distance, go to your basic psychic level (eyes open) and send a message, "Hello, my name is (your name) and I really would like to get to know you. I admire you very much and think you are an exciting person." Use whatever message you wish.

The above ideas can be used to meet anyone, not just a potential romantic interest.

In short order, you will get to know that person. Strange things will happen to bring it about. Some would say "coincidences" will occur, but I tell you, there is no such thing as coincidence. Every thing that happens is a direct result of some energy force causing it to happen. In these examples, it is your mental (psychic) thought energy that sets the process in motion and causes the "coincidence."

One caution about using your mental powers to bring a desired "love" into your life: be sure that is what you really want because it will happen, and you are going to have to live with the consequences.

■ ■

Chapter 16

COMMUNICATION WITH ENTITIES

If you have a special interest in entities (or ghosts, as most people refer to them) you will seek out opportunities to communicate with them. This is one of my special interests, and I take every opportunity I can to visit authentic haunted houses. I've had a lot of enjoyment, and have learned a lot, from communicating with entities.

Once you sincerely start to make contact, you will find that entities will start making contact with you even when you don't solicit it.

In addition, you can communicate with any deceased person you wish by inviting them into your mental awareness where you can experience intellectual contact.

Some contacts with entities may involve both a physical and a spiritual presence. This is something exciting. Many people are not that enthusiastic about such encounters. I am. If it titillates your fancy, go for it.

Case #23 _____

Encounter with a Ghost

I have had several encounters with entities over the years. I'll relate just one case that I found most interesting. I have changed the names of all persons involved to protect their privacy and feelings. The actual psychic encounter was exactly as I have written it here.

At the time I was working full-time as a sub-contract technical writer during the day. In the evenings and on weekends I worked as a professional hypnotherapist, building my skills and reputation.

Late one Sunday evening I received a phone call from Dr. Mansfield, who had trained me as a hypnotherapist and given me my certification.

"Lisa is dead, Bill. She was killed in a boating accident yesterday, and I need somebody to take over her clinic until we can get things settled. Will you do it?"

I explained that I was working full-time as a technical writer. She countered by offering me a substantial amount of money. I quit the writing job, and took over Lisa's hypnosis clinic on a temporary basis while legal matters were being settled.

I knew Lisa only by reputation; I had never met her. She had the most successful hypnosis clinic in the area. She had one employee, a receptionist, named Fern.

Fern refused to continue on with the clinic, despondent over Lisa's death. Fern had been with Lisa when the boating accident occurred and had been unable to save her from drowning.

I asked my wife to be my receptionist.

Lisa's estranged husband came in to claim some personal items that were not part of the business. He seemed like a nice person, but he certainly showed no remorse over Lisa's death. Even though he and Lisa had been separated for quite a few months, I thought he might have shown some feeling.

On Monday morning of the second week, we found a surprise waiting for us. All the drawers of the five-drawer file were open, and the contents were removed and scattered all over the floor. As far as we could tell, nothing was missing. Since we had the only key, and there were no signs of forced entry, we were perplexed.

The next day, books had been removed from the shelves and scattered.

The day after, my wife Dee and I were eating lunch in the office when we heard the outside door open and close. Dee walked out to greet the expected client, but no one was there. Again, some books were pulled from the shelf.

The following day was a repeat of the previous day. This time I ran outside to see who the prankster was. No one was there.

This kind of activity persisted off and on for several months. Dee said she was sure someone unseen was constantly watching her; she could feel it.

One day I noticed that the desk had a pullout type of writing board. I pulled it out for no particular reason and was stunned by what was taped to it. There were photographs of Lisa and Fern in embraces that disclosed that they were lovers. There also were love poems from one to the other which were quite sexually explicit. This explained Lisa's estrangement from her husband, his coolness toward her death, and Fern's depression over Lisa's death. I wondered if this was what our unseen visitor had been looking for.

From that moment on, we had no more visits from our unseen visitor until the day Dr. Mansfield phoned to tell me that effective the first of next month she had a new buyer for the clinic. The new owner was a woman named Maggie Johnson.

Later that day I rested on one of the recliners, closed my eyes and went to the Beach of Time to meditate while awaiting the arrival of my next client. Dee was out front minding the phone.

I heard the vinyl of the adjacent recliner squeak as though someone was sitting down in it. I knew no one had entered the room, so I mentally asked, "Who is there?"

"Lisa," was the mental reply I received.

"Why? What do you want?"

"I want you out of my clinic."

"Why?"

"Because you are a man.

"Haven't I been doing a good job?" I asked.

"Yes. You have done an excellent job, but you are a man and I want you out!"

"I will be leaving the end of the month for sure," I mentally replied. "Is that all right?"

"Fine. Who is taking your place?"

"The franchise has been purchased by a woman named Maggie Johnson."

"Maggie Johnson! I will not have that woman in my clinic. She is incompetent!"

"Lisa," I said, "you are dead. You have no purpose here now. Leave and find peace."

"I will not leave! This is my clinic. If Maggie Johnson takes over, I will see this place bankrupt in six months."

Then Lisa left, and I never personally encountered her again. But the story isn't over.

I phoned Dr. Mansfield and told her of the encounter with Lisa. She and a professional psychic came to the clinic. They both felt a powerful, negative presence. Their attempt to exorcise Lisa from the premises was unsuccessful.

In the few remaining days I had there, business just stopped. The final week I had only one client for one hour for a total cash intake of thirty-five dollars.

Then Maggie Johnson took over the franchise. No one came into the clinic; the phone never rang for appointments. She hung on for six months and had to declare bankruptcy.

Exercise #32

How to Contact Entities

To contact a deceased person, an angel, your Spirit Guide, or any entity, you can use either your basic psychic level or the Beach of Time. Try both ways to see which you prefer.

- Close your eyes and go to your basic psychic level.
- If you know what the entity looked like in life, visualize her/him.
- Invite the entity to enter your mental awareness by saying something like, "I ask my grandmother Adele Jones to kindly enter my mental awareness and communicate with me."
- Relax and allow the entity to make her/his/its presence known.
- If the entity does not make itself known, repeat the request.
- If the entity does not make itself known after about six requests, say, "I wish you had made yourself present to me, but I thank you anyway. Perhaps another time you will do so. I send you my love."
- When the entity does make itself known to you, say "Thank you for coming."

- Then proceed to converse with the entity just as when the entity was in body.
- When you are finished, say "I will say goodbye for now. I love you. Thank you for visiting with me. Please make your presence known to me anytime you wish."
- Then open your eyes in your usual manner.

The preceding exercise gives you a model from which to create your own procedure for communicating with entities. Depending on the circumstances, you would want to change the things you say to fit the situation.

Do not be timid about contacting entities. It really is not much different than contacting people or animals that are currently living. Remember, you are always protected by your psychic shield in case you encounter an unpleasant experience with an entity.

■ ■

Chapter 17

COMMUNICATION WITH ANIMALS

Animals only function at those states that we call altered states. They do not have a beta state of awareness. Therefore it is easy to communicate with them.

If you are a pet lover you do it all the time, whether you know it or not. Really skilled animal trainers do their work at a psychic level.

Case #11, Takra, in Chapter 7 is an especially good example of communicating with an animal.

If you wish to communicate with an animal, here is one exercise to get you started.

Exercise #33

Animal Communication

- Go to your basic psychic level with eyes open or closed, depending on the circumstances.
- Visualize the animal if it is not in your immediate view.
- If the animal has a name, mentally call it out in a gentle, friendly manner.
- If the animal does not have a name, just call out a description such as "The cow belonging to Mr. Brown that is lost."

- Tell the animal "I love you and respect you. I am your friend and will not harm you in any way."
- Then tell the animal what you want it to do.
- Keep your senses alert for any message or impressions the animal may be sending out.
- Continue interacting with the animal for as long as you wish.
- When you are finished, tell the animal "Thank you. I love you and I am your friend."
- Open your eyes, if they were closed.

The preceding exercise is a general guide. Modify it to suit your specific situation.

Using this procedure you should be able to establish a solid rapport with the animal. You could use the procedure for training, and also for finding lost pets.

As always, use your creative mind to assist you in using this or any other psychic procedure.

■ ■

Chapter 18

SOLVING PROBLEMS

Earlier in the book I said that when you boil it all down, use of psychic ability is about solving problems. The many case studies in this book, in one way or another, are about solving problems.

There are many ways to solve your daily problems using either your basic psychic level or The Beach of Time. Some methods will work better for you than others. So try a number of methods several times until you find what works best for you.

Here are four commonly used methods.

Exercise #34

Problem Solving Method #1

- Close your eyes.
- Go to your basic psychic level or to The Beach of Time.
- Visualize the unwanted situation as it exists.
- Study all of the details and then mentally say, "This is not what I want!"
- Immediately erase the picture completely and replace it with a picture of exactly what you do want.
- Study this new picture in detail and then mentally say, "This is what I want!"

159

- Then release the whole matter by saying, "I release this whole matter to higher mind for resolution."
- Open your eyes and go on about your business without dwelling on the problem any further.

Here is a common problem for which you might use this approach. You and your spouse have been quarreling and it is becoming serious. Visualize the quarreling, see the unhappy faces of yourself and your spouse, hear the harsh words, etc. Then, say you do not want this quarrel and erase the picture. Immediately create a picture of yourself and your spouse smiling, embracing, making love, talking kindly to each other, and so forth. Then release that picture to higher mind, saying that this is what you do want.

The results you get will be astounding.

Exercise #35

Problem Solving Method #2

- Close your eyes.
- Go to your basic psychic level or to the Beach of Time.
- Use your creative mind to fix the problem. For example, perhaps you have a cut that isn't healing as well as you would like. In your altered state of consciousness, remove the wound completely so that the area is covered with only healthy skin.
- Open your eyes and go on about your business. There are many variations on using your psychic ability for fixing anything.

Recall Case #10 in Chapter 7. I repaired my motor home under the most adverse conditions using my altered state of consciousness.

Exercise #36

Problem Solving Method #3

- Close your eyes.
- Contact your Spirit Guide by whatever method you were given in Exercise #30 in Chapter 14.
- Explain your problem to your Spirit Guide and ask for help in solving it.
- You may get an immediate solution, or you may just receive the awareness that help will be coming.
- When you are finished consulting, say "Thank you" to your Spirit Guide.
- Open your eyes and go on about your business without further concern about the problem.

I probably use this method more often than all other methods combined. Sometimes my Spirit Guide solves the problem for me. Other times my Spirit Guide gives me directions on how to solve the problem for myself.

Exercise #37

Problem Solving Method #4

You can sometimes solve problems using your nightly dreams.

- When you retire for the night, close your eyes and go to your basic psychic level.
- Mentally (or out loud) say, "Tonight I want to have a dream that will give me information that will help me solve my problem."
- Mentally state your problem.
- Mentally add, "I want to remember my dream when I awaken and I want to understand the meaning of the dream."
- Then just drift off to sleep.
- You will awaken either during the night or in the morning with a recollection of the dream and what it means in relation to your problem. Sometimes the meaning of your dream will pop into your head later in the day.

Using dreams can take some practice. It comes quite easily for some and is more difficult for others, so don't give up if you don't have a smashing success the first couple of times you try. Persistence will pay off.

The four methods I've just described for solving problems are not the only methods available, but they will do nicely in most situations. You may develop your own methods as you progress.

Chapter 19

YOUR WARNING SYSTEM

Your mind has the ability to warn you of imminent danger even though you are not consciously aware that the danger exists.

All you need to do is to go to your basic psychic level or to the Beach of Time and program in the warning signal that you want your Guardian Angel or Spirit Guide to give you to alert you of imminent danger.

A friend of mine is warned by a flashing red light in his mind. Another one becomes extremely cold. Decide how you want to be warned and program it in using the exercise I will describe later in this chapter.

Case #24 _____

My Warning System

On the Beach of Time I had asked my Guardian Angel to warn me in whatever way was most appropriate for the situation. It saved my life once. Here is what happened.

I was driving about forty miles per hour on a busy street. My right foot, as though driven by a mind of its own, quickly jerked from the accelerator and slammed down hard on the brake pedal, bringing me to a complete, emergency stop.

At that instant, a car shot out at high speed from a blind side street, running the stop sign in the process. He crossed just inches in front of me. Had I not stopped, there is no doubt that I would have been hit and probably killed.

It took me a few moments to recover my senses and assess the situation. I could not see down the side street from my position on the boulevard because of heavy foliage.

There was no way I could have seen the speeding car approach, and I knew beyond doubt that I had not braked the car. For that brief period, some force other than my own will had operated my right leg.

I immediately went to my basic psychic level and said, "Thank you" to my Guardian Angel.

Exercise #38

Programming Your Own Warning System

- Close your eyes.
- Go to the Beach of Time and summon your Guardian Angel to be with you.
- Ask your Guardian Angel to warn you of impending danger in whatever way is most appropriate. Or request a specific kind of warning, such as a light flashing in your mind, a sudden tenseness, or whatever would catch your attention.
- Tell your Guardian Angel, "Thank you."
- Leave the Beach of Time and open your eyes.

Don't leave home without your warning system programmed into your psychic mind.

You only need to do it once, and it will last for life.

However, if you are a person who always checks the door locks two or three times before leaving the house, you may feel more comfortable programming in your warning system as often as you wish.

Chapter 20

PSYCHIC TRAFFIC CONTROL

Have you ever been driving on the Interstate highway system and become annoyed because someone driving slowly in the fast lane was holding you up? Well, I have and here is how I handled it.

Case #25
Moving Cars Out of the Way

Several years ago my wife and I had the need to drive to a city over a hundred miles from our home once every week. The highway was always crowded, making it a long, tedious drive.

One day I said to my wife, "Hon, today you drive and I will move all the cars out of the way." Predictably, she thought I had a couple of screws loose. "You just get in the fast lane and stay there," I assured her, "and I will keep the road clear in front of you." Being a good sport, she agreed to try it.

Within seconds after she pulled onto the highway into the fast lane she rapidly approached a car. I altered my state of consciousness to my basic psychic level (eyes open, of course) and addressed the driver something like this, "Sir, I would be very grateful if you would kindly pull into the right lane and let us pass because we have an urgent need to get where we are going. Thank you."

He immediately pulled into the right lane. I mentally thanked him again as we passed.

I moved one hundred percent of the vehicles out of our way that day. Once during a clear stretch of road I dozed off, only to be awakened by my wife poking me in the ribs and saying, "Wake up. There is a truck about half a mile ahead of me." My wife was having so much fun that she wanted to drive on the return trip.

After doing this a few times while my wife drove, I decided to see if I could drive and move vehicles at the same time. It worked every time.

In nearly nine months of making those weekly trips there was only one vehicle that did not immediately respond. This story is worth telling, because it illustrates an important part of psychic work.

I was driving and an eighteen-wheeler was in front of me. I mentally projected to the driver as usual, but the driver did not respond at all. I repeated my request several more times, but still received no response.

Just as I was wondering why, the truck had a blowout and began to swerve all over the road. Fortunately, the driver eventually brought the truck to a safe stop on the right shoulder of the road, but not before executing some terrifying swerves into both lanes.

If he had pulled over to allow me to pass as I had mentally requested, I would have been alongside him when he had the blowout and there is no doubt that his truck would have slammed into my car on my wife's side.

Higher mind had taken care of me because I did not have the awareness to take care of myself. Apparently my mental transmission had been blocked by higher mind, to protect me. Do you see now why 1 had you create a shield of protection in Chapter 5?

This mental exercise of moving vehicles out of the way greatly sharpened my telepathic sending abilities, and most importantly, it taught me how to function effectively at a psychic level with my eyes open while actively doing something else.

Exercise #39

Moving Vehicles Psychically

- Go to your basic psychic level with your eyes open.
- If you know the gender of the driver in front of you, address her/him appropriately as Ma'am or Sir.
- If you don't know the person's gender say something like, "Driver of the red Mustang" or other words of your choice, to contact the driver.
- Your entire mental conversation would go something like this: "Sir, I have an urgent need to pass you and you are blocking my way. I would greatly appreciate it if you would safely move to the other traffic lane for a few moments to allow me to safely pass. Thank you."
- When you are passing the vehicle mentally say, "Thank you, sir. I appreciate it." If you can catch her/his attention, you should also smile and nod your head.

That is all there is to it. Of course, I highly recommend that you have previously programmed your psychic shield and your warning system to prevent an accident.

■ ■

Chapter 21

PSYCHIC WAKE-UP CALL

Here is a practical use of your mind that is also excellent for sharpening your psychic abilities. When you go to sleep, direct your psychic mind to awaken you at a precise time.

The following exercise explains how you do it.

Exercise #40

Wake-Up Call

- When you go to bed, close your eyes and go to your basic psychic level.
- Visualize a clock.
- Set the clock to the time at which you want to awaken. Your choice might be 7:00 A.M.
- Mentally reaffirm, "This is the exact time I want to awaken, 7:00 A.M."
- Then drift off to sleep.
- In the morning you will awaken quite suddenly. Immediately look at the clock. The time should be 7:00 A.M. (or whatever time you had chosen to set on your mental clock).
- If you have awakened within five minutes or less of the time you wanted, consider this an accurate response from your psychic mind.

- Immediately close your eyes briefly and say, "Thank you. This is the accuracy and responsiveness I desire in all my psychic work."
- Then open your eyes and go about your day's activities.
- If your mental clock was more than five minutes off, do not accept that as being sufficiently accurate because that is a sloppy psychic response. Your mind is capable of accuracy, and you must insist upon it.
- First, check the accuracy of your clock. I once awakened three minutes later than I should have, according to the clock (I insist on better accuracy than that). I dialed the Bureau of Standards and discovered that my clock was three minutes fast. My mind had been accurate. Don't "chew out" your mind until you have checked your clock.
- If your clock is accurate, alter your consciousness and say, "I am pleased that I was awakened. However, this is not the degree of accuracy that I demand for my psychic work. I want complete accuracy from now on. When I set my psychic wake-up call I want to awaken exactly at the time I have chosen. I will not tolerate sloppy results."
- Then open your eyes and go about your business. Later, when you go to bed, set your psychic wake-up call once again. Repeat this process nightly until you are satisfied with consistent, accurate results.

You can also modify this procedure to alert you to keep appointments or schedules during the day. To do this, follow the above procedure except that, instead of telling your mind to wake you, tell it to alert you at a certain time during the day by flashing a light in your mind, forcing you to look at your watch, causing a buzzing in your ears, or through some other method of your choice. Be creative.

Chapter 22

FINDING A PARKING SPACE

After my success with moving cars, I decided to reserve parking spaces for myself. I really didn't mind having to walk some distance from my car to wherever I was going (I like the exercise); I just wanted to see if I could do it.

Case #26

Reserving My Parking Space

Before I would leave home I would alter my state of consciousness to my basic psychic level and visualize the parking space nearest to the door of the building to which I was going (supermarket, work, etc.).

I would visualize the space as being empty, with a sign on it that read, "Reserved for Bill Hewitt."

Guess what? It worked one hundred percent of the time.

Then I started to get fancy. I would reserve the third space from the door, or the fifth, or whatever other location in the parking lot I preferred. And that worked one hundred percent of the time, too.

I stopped doing this after a few months simply because I wasn't that interested in saving a few steps, but it really sharpened my visualization and psychic abilities.

Try it for yourself. The following exercise will show you how. It is fun and excellent practice for your psychic development.

Exercise #41

Reserving Your Parking Space

- Close your eyes.
- Go to your basic psychic level.
- Visualize the parking space you want to have available to you when you arrive at the place you are intending to visit.
- Visualize that parking space as being empty.
- Mentally identify the location of the space. For example, think of the first space in the third row from Walnut Street in the Wal-Mart parking lot.
- Mentally place a sign in that parking space that reads, "Reserved for (Your Name)."
- Say "Thank you" to higher mind.
- Open your eyes, proceed to your destination and park your car in your reserved space.

You can try other variations on the same theme. Have all of the traffic lights be green for you, or reserve a seat for yourself at a movie or sports event. You get the idea. Be creative as you exercise your psychic abilities.

■ ■

Chapter 23

No Dozing Control

Have you ever gotten drowsy or even dozed off briefly at the wheel while driving on a long trip?

You can use your psychic mind to solve this problem.

Exercise #42

Staying Awake

- When you feel yourself becoming groggy or drowsy, immediately pull onto the shoulder of the road, stop, and turn off your vehicle's engine.
- Turn on your warning flashers (if it is dark) so that other vehicles can see you.
- Close your eyes and go to your basic psychic level.
- Ask your Guardian Angel to watch over you and keep you awake until you are safely at your destination. You must be specific about your destination. You might say something like, "... until I am safely at my home and in bed," or, "... until I am in my motel room." Do not speak in general terms, such as, "... until I reach St. Louis." I will explain further in a moment.
- Remain at your basic psychic level with your eyes closed for a short time; rest for five to fifteen minutes as you choose.

- Then mentally give yourself a suggestion such as, "I am now completely rested, as if I have just had four hours of deep, relaxing sleep. In a few moments I am going to open my eyes and be wide awake and alert. I will remain awake and alert until I reach (state your specific destination)."
- Open your eyes and continue your trip.

There is an important reason that you should not use a general description of your destination in this exercise.

If you say, "... until I reach St. Louis," your mind will allow you to go to sleep the moment you reach the St. Louis city limits. You could be driving at fifty-five miles per hour (or perhaps faster) when you reach the St. Louis city limits, still many miles from your intended destination. That is no time to fall asleep.

You must be specific with the directions you give your mind.

You can use this method whenever you need to remain awake and alert for a while longer, such as when you are listening to a lecture. I've used it many times to stay awake while writing late into the night.

■ ■

Chapter 24

Skill Improvement

We all have skills that we would like to improve, be it typing, sports, driving, quilting, cooking, speaking, writing, or whatever interests you.

Your psychic mind can help you to improve a great deal.

Exercise #43

Improving Your Skills at Anything

- Close your eyes
- Go to either your basic psychic level or to the Beach of Time, as you prefer.
- Visualize yourself perfectly performing the skill you are working on.
- See yourself as relaxed, yet completely alert and happy as you perfectly perform the skill.
- Take a couple of minutes to fix the picture of your perfect performance in your mind.
- Then mentally say, "This is what I want higher mind to enable me to achieve: to become the best (name the skill) that I am capable of becoming."
- Open your eyes.

Your improved skill will become reality in the physical world. Depending on the skill, of course, this could take some time.

For example, what if your tennis game isn't what you want it to be?

Visualize yourself playing a perfect game. Do this daily and watch how your game does, indeed, improve. Keep up the visualization, along with continuing to play the game, until your performance is where you want it to be.

This does not mean that you can visualize yourself doing something you have never done before and instantly become an expert. Not at all. Visualization will help you to improve a skill you already possess, or it will help you to learn a new skill. But visualization will not just give the skill to you without any effort on your part.

Remember: in order to become reality, desire must always be followed by constructive action. There are no free rides.

■ ■

Chapter 25

READING/STUDYING

Your psychic ability gives you a superior way to read or study and retain and understand what you have just studied. The method is quite simple.

Exercise #44

Superior Comprehension

- Close your eyes.
- Go to your basic psychic level or to the Beach of Time.
- Mentally say, "In a few moments I am going to open my eyes and read (name of item you are going to read). I will have superior comprehension of what I read and I will be able to recall anything I read whenever I wish."
- Then open your eyes and read.
- When you are finished reading, close your eyes and say, "I have just read (name of item). I have superior comprehension of the material and I can recall it whenever I wish."
- Open your eyes and go about the rest of your activities for the day.

You have locked in the information for future use whenever you need it.

You can also use this method for listening to a lecture so that you will have greater recall and comprehension of the information you hear.

Continued Study

Now that you have a procedure for using your psychic ability to give you deeper comprehension, you may want to think about pursuing further psychic and/or occult study after you finish this book.

Life, if lived to the fullest, is a constant quest for knowledge. So yes, continue to study, but with one proviso: study judiciously.

What does it mean to study judiciously?

In the introduction to this book I said that there are many people who know the price of everything and the value of nothing. Such people are like the ivory tower professors we have all heard about who can quote every date, name, and event since the dawn of history, but are unable to perform such simple tasks as making reservations and purchasing tickets to visit the places they know so much about.

The pursuit of learning can be pointless, if you allow it to be. I know people who relentlessly pursue every course of study available that has anything to do with psychic phenomena, hypnosis, astral travel, dreams, telepathy, etc. They can hardly wait for one class or book to end so that they can start another. They read all of the "in" books on every psychic subject. They have read about Rolfing, Rebirthing, Out-of-Body Travel, all of Edgar Cayce's books, and on and on. These people are terrific conversationalists at parties. Yet with all of this "learning" they are unable to perform the simplest of psychic tasks, to alter their state of consciousness at will and achieve some psychic goal.

The irony is that the courses and books were all worthwhile. Then why didn't these individuals learn? Because learning is not a pursuit, it is a process that starts deep within self.

It is in the context of process that I will now discuss your further study.

With this book you have brought yourself into the realm of the psychic world. But, at this moment, you don't realize or understand the full scope of the skills and knowledge you have at your command. You cannot possibly know these things until you begin to use your newfound psychic abilities every day. Therefore, your next logical learning experience should be to learn by doing.

For the time being, I recommend that you put additional formal psychic study and classes on the back burner. There are various religions, cults, and organizations that have their own teachings for psychic development and use, which provide good courses of study. For now, give yourself a fair chance to develop and use what you have learned from this book before jumping into further studies.

I estimate that you should wait at least one year before pursuing further formal study.

There are many roads to psychic development and practice. If you keep switching roads you end up doing a lot of traveling, but you may not reach your destination. Or at least, it may take you much longer to reach your destination.

In the meantime, do some casual reading to augment your daily psychic practice. The idea now is to allow yourself to experience and learn at the rate that is best for you. If you try to force yourself too far or too quickly, you could end up actually setting yourself back.

If I were to suggest a typical plan for you to follow, it might look something like this:

1. Use your psychic powers, starting today and continuing every day from now on. Use everything you have learned in this book, and give yourself a chance to create other psychic practices on your own as your abilities develop.

2. After about two months of pure practice, as described above, select a book of your choice and casually read it. Continue with your daily psychic practice, of course. Since each of you is unique, the reading selection that is best for you is unique. As a generalization, a good starter book could be *Hypnosis* (Llewellyn Publications; William W. Hewitt, author) or perhaps the booklet *As a Man Thinketh* (DeVorss & Co.; James Allen, author).

3. Allow at least a month to pass after finishing your first book before selecting another book to read casually. Of course, continue daily psychic practice. A couple of books I read at about this time were *Psycho-Cybernetics* (Wilshire Book Co.; Maxwell Maltz, author) and *Wisdom of the Mystic Masters* (Parker Publishing Co.; Joseph Weed, author). You will probably find some more recent works to your liking.

4. Continue to select books that interest you, allowing at least one month between finishing one book and starting another.

5. After a year or so of self-development of your psychic powers, you can determine for yourself whether or not you wish further formal training. You will probably have

an awareness by this time concerning your future course of action. If not, ask your Spirit Guide or Guardian Angel for advice.

Probably ninety percent of you (my guess) will not want or need further formal study because you will have discovered how to learn and grow through your own developed faculties.

Some years ago my Spirit Guide told me to stop formal studying and to use the skills and knowledge I already possessed. It was great advice, and I took it. I now learn through my own psychic faculties, occasionally augmented with casual reading. My psychic faculties even lead me to what I need to read, when I need to read it.

By following these five steps you will make psychic practice part of your everyday way of life in every facet of your life. That is where you need to be.

Then you will begin to know the value, and not just the price, of everything.

■ ■

Chapter 26

SUMMARY AND A
LOOK FORWARD

Using your psychic abilities is a way of life. No longer are you bound to the traditional ways by which you used to live. Now you have an instantly available ability to live your life in the fullest and most exciting way possible. There is virtually no situation that you cannot handle easily, smoothly, and satisfactorily. It works!

Sensitize yourself to be constantly alert for opportunities to use every psychic trick you have up your sleeve. It doesn't necessarily have to be some gigantic project that you direct your energies toward, although it certainly can be.

Perhaps you hear on the radio that a gunman is holed up in your city, and he has hostages. Use your psychic ability to project to that gunman; talk sensibly to him at the psychic level so that he will not harm anyone. Project courage and protection to the hostages.

What if you aren't certain how to go about some demanding task that your boss has asked you to perform? Use your psychic abilities to find out what to do. Solve the problem in your mind, and then do the work as your mind directs you. Problem solved!

You might see a child crying on the street. If you are not able to stop and physically help the child, then send help and comfort at a psychic level.

I am not advocating using psychic help as a cop-out so that you don't have to render physical aid. Never. You should always offer physical help whenever possible. There are thousands of times, however, when you just are not able to help physically. In those cases, use your psychic abilities.

Now that you have committed yourself to a new way of life, there is one final piece advice I want to impress on you.

Don't become impressed with yourself. Don't go around announcing to the world or to whoever will listen, "I am a psychic. Let me butt into your business."

I give this advice because I personally know psychics who have become quite egotistical and self-centered. I have seen psychics lose their abilities because they begin to think that they are the source of power.

The only source of power is the supreme source that created everything. You have the privilege of being a channel for the expression of that power.

As for the cry, "I am a psychic!" — so what? So is everyone, potentially. Big deal. You have merely learned how to use some of the abilities given to you as a birthright by your Creator. There's no need to get big-headed about it.

Live your life in quiet happiness, using your psychic ability to create a better world for yourself.

Your life is already beginning to change for the better in some measure.

If you continue to exercise your psychic ability every day, even if only for brief moments, the changes will continue to occur and become more profound. You are the entire play, the script writer, the actor, the stage manager, and the director. You make happen the things that you want to have happen. Your success rate is directly proportional to your efforts, persistence, perseverance, belief, expectancy, intensity, and openness to experience and learning.

There are a number of thing you will notice happening as you become more and more in one with your higher mind. You will have experiences that come in a flash of total awareness that nearly defies adequate description. This is because our vocabulary is designed for the physical world we are temporarily residing in, and these experiences are non-physical. Hence, at best our physical-world words only partially embrace the needs of describing a non-physical world.

If you experience music in the psychic realm, it will be so extraordinarily profound and beautiful that you will be unable to adequately express it in words. You will see things in mental images. You will hear things in non-verbal sounds. You will gain a total awareness of something in a split second; it may take several hours to verbally explain the information you received in that flash, and even then, you will find your explanation falling short of what you know in your mind.

Some years ago, while in meditation, I was given total awareness of reincarnation. Up until that moment I had not read anything about reincarnation. I had not given the subject any thought. I just was not interested in it.

In this particular meditation session, I was not seeking any information about reincarnation, but I was given the information in an instant. I am not able to adequately explain in words the inner understanding and knowledge I have of the subject. The information came as a total awareness; that is the best description I am able to give. When you have your own experiences, you will understand what I am trying to say.

Another thing you will notice is that you are subtly directed into a different circle of acquaintances and relationships. Those whom you can help will be drawn to you, or you to them. Those who can help you are drawn to you, or you to them. You will quickly be weaned from potentially detrimental people and relationships. After some period of time, you will look back and find that those who were once central in your life are no longer important. Your life will have taken on a dimension that you could not have predicted.

Your entire value system will change. Things that used to get you uptight will not even cause you to pause. Alcohol will not be important to you, if it ever was. You may have an occasional drink, but if you never had one you wouldn't care.

You quite likely will find cigarettes and smoke repulsive. This is due, in part at least, to the fact that you will be operating more and more in an altered state of mind, both deliberately and spontaneously. In an altered state you become extremely sensitive. Thus, smoke and cigarettes become great irritants, and can cause physical discomfort. When I am in an altered state (which is most of the time), cigarettes or smoke anywhere near me cause me to experience throat congestion, swelling inside my nose that blocks my breathing, and severe coughing.

It is quite likely that you will become a loner, in the sense that you will be independent and free. You will not feel bonded to groups or rules. No one will make your decisions for you. Yet at the same time you will feel a very real spiritual bond with everyone and everything. You will see your responsibilities clearly, and you will see the responsibilities of others clearly.

It is as though you see all people as individual universes. Each is a tiny bubble floating through space under its own power and direction. Every so often two of these bubbles come together, and like bubbles, they blend and overlap.

They may blend for a very short period of time, or for a long time. While blended, these bubbles share certain portions of themselves with one another while still maintaining their own identities and autonomy. At some point, the bubbles separate and float on to experience other bubbles. The same bubbles may come together for a while, then float apart for a while, then rejoin again, and so on.

So it is with you and your interactions with others. You give experience to, and gain experience from, others. But you and they still remain the masters of your own universes, and set the course for your own learning and spiritual growth. It is impossible to give without also receiving.

The following personal example may help put some of this into perspective.

Case #27
What Goes Around, Comes Around

Some years ago, I helped a woman (through hypnosis) to get rid of her smoking habit. She had limited funds, so I did it for just fifteen percent of my usual fee. Then she went on her way, out of my life.

About five years had passed before I got a phone call from the woman. She was terminally ill and in the final months of her life. She was also financially destitute, but she needed help.

During her final months I gave her much time, freely, doing what I could to ease her pain, help her understand the nature of death, and overcome her fears.

She died. I felt that my efforts had been inadequate, but didn't know what more I could have done. In the process of helping her, however, I received profound revelations of understanding and knowledge, and another payoff was yet to come.

Even though I felt I had not done much to help her, she must have felt otherwise.

A few months after her death I got a phone call from a local cable television program producer who had been a longtime friend of the lady who had died. On her deathbed, she had talked to her producer friend; her conversation was almost exclusively about me and the great help I had been. The TV producer was quite moved by the experience and got in touch with me.

The result: I was offered a paid speaking engagement. The kicker is that my first book was forthcoming, and this gave me the opportunity to plug the work.

I could relate additional such personal experiences, but that isn't necessary to make the point: *What goes around, comes around.* You generate positive energy, and positive energy comes back to you in some way at some time.

Conversely, if you generate negative energy, that too will return to you — count on it! There is no such thing as coincidence. Coincidence doesn't exist. Coincidence is one example of a physical-world word used to describe a nonphysical-world experience; a woefully inadequate and inappropriate word? People use the word "coincidence" to describe an event they don't understand. As a psychic, you will understand.

Understand one thing clearly, right now. Do not use your psychic abilities to help someone with the intent of receiving an ultimate reward. Such an intent is the wrong reason to offer help, and it may generate negative energy which will be counterproductive to the result you expect.

Use your power to help simply because you can do it and there is a need. Just the knowledge that you did what you could is reward enough. Period. Then forget the matter and go on to other things. This will become an automatic response for you as you become more and more ingrained in the nonphysical world.

You will not always be aware of the chain of actions that lead to an experience. Don't concern yourself about it. If you need to know, you will. In the example I just gave about the lady I helped, the chain of actions was quite evident. Most experiences are not that clearly delineated to your conscious awareness. That is why it is important to program your goals for end results, not for the specific interim steps you think are necessary to achieve the goals.

Years ago I programmed myself to become a successful writer. I reinforced that goal daily. I made it, but the winding, twisty, unpredictable path I walked to get there was incredible. At any given time, it seemed highly unlikely that I was on the right path at all. Then suddenly the cloud lifted and everything fell into perspective.

The unlikely path I had followed was exactly the right one and brought rewards and experiences far beyond anything I had originally dreamed. If I had tried to program the exact path to follow, I wouldn't have had the insight to choose the one I did follow, and consequently would not have realized my goal, or experienced all of the life-enriching events I encountered along the way. Fortunately, I had merely programmed for the goal, and thus gained a life experience that I would not trade with anyone, for any amount of wealth.

Each of us is an immense energy source in an infinite ocean of immense energy. This is all intelligent energy. Our awareness embraces many levels. All of the knowledge, intelligence, and energy is available to us. Energy in and of itself is neither good nor bad; it just is. How we use it can be good or detrimental — that is our choice.

Once we execute a choice, it is irrevocable, and we must deal with the results either now or later, in this life or in another living experience. That's the Law.

Remember, the Law of Being discussed in an earlier chapter states: "whatever comes to you, whatever happens to you, whatever surrounds you, will be in accordance with your consciousness, and nothing else; whatever is in your consciousness must happen, no matter who tries to stop it; and whatever is not in your consciousness cannot possibly happen."

It behooves us then to make positive, beneficial, constructive choices. Use your psychic ability to go within and consult with higher self in order to determine the best choices for you to make. You will receive the guidance you need. Just be sure to listen and follow that small, still voice within, rather than rationalize another course of action.

These things will become crystal clear to you via your own inner awareness as you become more and more in tune with self at all levels of self — hence, oneness.

Ah Ha! Oneness! Is that what this is all about, oneness? No. This is merely the beginning of what oneness is about. The rest you must find out and experience for yourself in your own way, at your own pace, in your own time. The important thing is that your journey has begun, and it is an exciting one.

I tell you these things to serve as signposts along your journey, so that you will be better equipped to make better choices.

There will be times when it seems as if you are not progressing or are even slipping backward. This is temporary and necessary, although you may not see why at the time. Just stick to your beliefs and goals. The sun always rises and always prevails over the clouds, which are temporary.

We are here on earth as part of our spiritual growth experience, to learn, to contribute, to be happy, and to achieve. We are in school, so to speak. So attend your classes, pay attention, do your homework, and look forward to passing into the next grade, and the next, until you graduate from the school of life.

I detect a growing awareness. You are getting a gleam in your eyes. You have the birth of an understanding. Your understanding is still an infant, but it is there and growing. You are beginning to have some insight as to who you really are. Who we all are. What life is all about. Where you are going in this earthly existence. Where you are going ultimately.

I am not going to spell it out for you any more specifically than I have. To do so would take the edge off your own experience, and I don't want to do that.

There really is no viable excuse for not using the psychic ability you were given when you were created to the fullest extent of your awareness. You know now that you have some measure of ability. You also know now how to develop and use it. All that remains to be done is to do it.

The brief case histories presented in this book illustrate some of the things that can be done with proper use of psychic power. As you venture into the magnificent world of the psychic, you will catalog your own encounters.

I want to prepare you for one type of experience you will encounter more often than you want to — the failure experience.

You will not always succeed at what you want, and often you will not know why.

Case #28 ————————————————————————
Two Failures

#1 — A young woman phoned me one evening, asking for help. Several years earlier I had done some psychic readings, quite successfully, for her and some of her friends. Now she had a serious problem. Her two-year-old daughter had been kidnapped. She and her ex-husband were involved in a bitter custody battle, and she suspected that he had taken the child. She wanted to know where the child was, if she was safe, etc. I tried daily for two weeks and drew an absolute blank every time. I was not able to help her one iota, and felt poorly about it.

#2 — I have had several people die in spite of my help. These were people who had already been declared terminally ill by their physicians, before I got involved. I was not tampering with their health or playing doctor. I was just trying to do what the doctors said could not be done. In those cases, the physicians were right.

When you get accustomed to dealing in the psychic realm, you begin to think that you can always rectify anything in the manner that you choose. This is not so. There is a much higher intelligence than ours, and we must defer to it. It is not our role to know everything or achieve everything in this life experience just because we want to. Our role is to do our best, offer our services with integrity, and make our mightiest effort to enrich lives and the world. Within the framework designed by higher intelligence, we will succeed. Higher intelligence does not expect more than that from you, and you should not expect more than that from yourself.

When your efforts are unsuccessful within the framework you want, do not become discouraged. Know that higher mind knows better, and you are working within higher mind's framework rather than the one you perceive.

Then forget the matter, and go on to continue offering your best efforts wherever you find the opportunity.

We are all born with innate tendencies that can be developed into fine skills if we study, practice, and are diligent in our efforts. There are some things for which we have a natural ability, and some for which we have little, or limited ability. If we concentrate on developing and using our natural abilities, we can achieve great things in those areas. If we concentrate on those things for which we have little or no natural ability, we may see some small improvement, but are highly unlikely to make any significant achievement.

For example, I have almost no natural ability for carpentry work. You could send me to school for a year to study carpentry, and I would probably learn to saw wood a little better and to hit my thumb with a hammer less frequently, but I still would not be able to build a decent-looking wooden box.

However, I have a natural writing ability, and I quickly learned to write professionally acceptable books, articles, and stories.

The same is true in developing and using your mind in special ways. You will discover certain psychic abilities that are natural for you, and others for which you have limited ability. The exercises, case studies, and tutorial information in this book enable you to take your first major step toward unleashing your natural psychic abilities.

Concentrate on those things that come the easiest and feel the most natural to you. Of course you can concentrate on things that aren't easy or natural if you wish, but you should realize that you may fall short of your expectations. Falling short of your expectations is not failure. None of us are able to achieve great success at everything; we wouldn't be human if we could.

The most successful way to achieve failure is to not try.

So I do urge you to try everything in this book, and to create your own procedures and try them. Keep on exploring and expanding your psychic mind.

Be content and happy with your successes and give thanks to higher mind.

Do not be discouraged with your non-successes; they are also part of your learning process.

Give thanks for all your experiences, whether smashing successes or dismal non-successes, and go forward for the rest of your life with an open, creative mind, using your innate psychic ability to create a fulfilling life for yourself and for others with whom you interact.

My blessings go with you.

■ ■

Astral Projection for Beginners

Edain McCoy

Enter a world in which time and space have no meaning or influence. This is the world of the astral plane, an ethereal, unseen realm often perceived as parallel to and interpenetrating our physical world. *Astral Projection for Beginners* shows you how to send your consciousness at will to these other places, then bring it back with full knowledge of what you have experienced.

Explore the misconceptions and half-truths that often impede the beginner, and create a mental atmosphere in which you become free to explore the universe both inside and outside your consciousness. This book offers six different methods for you to try: general transfer of consciousness, projecting through the chakras, meditating towards astral separation, guided meditation, using symbolic gateways, and stepping out of your dreams. Ultimately you will be able to condition your mind to allow you to project at will.

1-56718-625-4, 256 pp., 5 ¼ x 8, softcover   *$9.95*

Hypnosis for Beginners

William W. Hewitt

Hypnosis is one of the most valuable tools available for the enrichment of lives. It's a normal, safe, healthy phenomenon that brings you to the altered state of consciousness needed for directing your mind to specific goals. The power and scope of self-hypnosis can blow your mind into new, heightened levels of awareness and achievement.

When you are finished with this step-by-step guide, you will be able to hypnotize yourself and others safely and easily. Whether your goal is to stop smoking, control migraine headaches or commune with your spirit guides, you will find hypnosis routines that you can use for any purpose, including special tips for hypnosis with children. In addition, you will be able to record your own audiotapes to regress yourself into past lives. Several case histories from the author's own clientele dramatically illustrate the power of this remarkably simple yet profound technique.

1-56718-359-X, 288 pp., 5 ³⁄₁₆ x 8, softcover   *$9.95*

Astral Travel for Beginners
Transcend Time and Space with Out-of-Body Experiences
Richard Webster

Astral projection, or the out-of-body travel, is a completely natural experience. You have already astral traveled thousands of times in your sleep, you just don't remember it when you wake up. Now, you can learn how to leave your body at will, be fully conscious of the experience, and remember it when you return.

The exercises in this book are carefully graded to take you step-by-step through an actual out-of-body experience. Once you have accomplished this, it becomes easier and easier to leave your body. That's why the emphasis in this book is on your first astral travel.

The ability to astral travel can change your life. You will have the freedom to go anywhere and do anything. You can explore new worlds, go back and forth through time, make new friends, and even find a lover on the astral planes. Most importantly, you will find that you no longer fear death as you discover that you are indeed a spiritual being independent of your physical body.

1-56718-796-x, 256 pp., 5 ³/₁₆ x 8   *$9.95*

Self Hypnosis for a Better Life

William W. Hewitt

The sound of your own voice is an incredibly powerful tool for speaking to and reprogramming your subconscious. Now, for the first time, you can select your own self-hypnosis script and record it yourself. *Self-Hypnosis for a Better Life* gives the exact wording for 23 unique situations that can be successfully handled with self-hypnosis. Each script is complete in itself and only takes 30 minutes to record. You simply read the script aloud into a tape recorder, then replay the finished tape back to yourself and reap the rewards of self-hypnosis!

Whether you want to eradicate negativity from your life, attract a special romantic partner, solve a problem, be more successful at work, or simply relax, you will find a number of tapes to suit your needs. Become your own hypnotherapist as you design your own self-improvement program, and you can make anything happen.

1-56718-358-1, 256 pp., 5 3/16 x 8, illus., softcover   *$9.95*

Write Your Own Magic
The Hidden Powers in your Words

Richard Webster

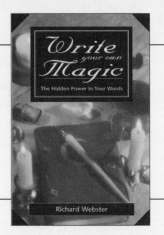

Write your innermost dreams and watch them come true! This book will show you how to use the incredible power of words to create the life that you have always dreamed about. We all have desires, hopes and wishes. Sadly, many people think theirs are unrealistic or unattainable. Write Your Own Magic shows you how to harness these thoughts by putting them to paper.

Once a dream is captured in writing it becomes a goal, and your subconscious mind will find ways to make it happen. From getting a date for Saturday night to discovering your purpose in life, you can achieve your goals, both small and large. You will also learn how to speed up the entire process by making a ceremony out of telling the universe what it is you want. With the simple instructions in this book, you can send your energies out into the world and magnetize all that is happiness, success, and fulfillment to you.

0-7387-0001-0, 312 pp., 5 ³/₁₆ x 8, illus.   *$9.95*

Success Secrets:
Letters to Matthew

Richard Webster

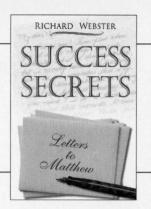

Rekindle your passion for your life's work.

Matthew is lacking vision and passion in his life. His marriage is on the rocks and his boss is worried about Matthew's falling sales figures. Just as he is feeling the lowest he has felt in years, he goes to his mailbox and finds an envelope addressed to him, with no return address and no stamp. He instantly recognizes the handwriting as that of his old history teacher from high school. Wouldn't Mr. Nevin be dead by now? Why would Matthew get a letter from him after thirty years?

The letter and the others that follow are the backbone of this little book. Each one gives Matthew encouragement and new ways to deal with his life. After the seventh letter, Matthew sets out to find Mr. Nevin and thank him personally. Mr. Nevin's daughter in-law answers the door, and explains to Matthew that Mr. Nevin passed away five years previously. As the story ends, Matthew ponders the origin of the letters.

This little book is a quick read about following your dreams, setting goals, overcoming obstacles, pushing yourself even further, and making work fun.

1-56718-788-9, 168 pp., 5 ³⁄₁₆ x 8   *$7.95*

To order, call 1-877-NEW-WRLD
Prices subject to change without notice